FRIENDSHIP AND THE MORAL LIFE

Friendship and the Moral Life

PAUL J. WADELL, C.P.

UNIVERSITY OF NOTRE DAME PRESS
NOTRE DAME, INDIANA

Copyright © 1989
University of Notre Dame
Notre Dame, Indiana 46556
www.undpress.nd.edu
All Rights Reserved

Manufactured in the United States of America

Reprinted in 1993, 1998, 2003, 2007, 2009

Library of Congress Cataloging-in-Publication Data
Wadell, Paul J.
    Friendship and the moral life / Paul J. Wadell.
        p.   cm.
    Includes index.
    ISBN 0-268-00973-2 (cl.)
    ISBN-13: 978-0-268-00974-8 (pbk.)
    ISBN-10: 0-268-00974-0 (pbk.)
    1. Friendship.   2. Friendship—Religious aspects—
Christianity.   3. Christian ethics—Catholic authors.   I. Title.
BJ 1533.F8W33   1989
241'.676—dc20   89-40022

To My Mother and Father

Contents

Foreword

I was not much beyond my own graduate student days when I discovered I was to teach a Ph.D. seminar at the University of Notre Dame. Unsure how or what I should teach, in desperation I organized a seminar around readings from Aristotle, Aquinas, Kant, and Barth. I was not sure what such a course would do but I was sure that anyone who wanted to become a theologian concerned with matters ethical should wrestle with these positions. I had the feeling that you would not come out of that course with many answers but you would certainly know where many of the problems were. In truth, I had some vague intuitions about how these texts might illumine one another—for example, how friendship as a constitutive element of Aristotle's account of moral rationality would starkly contrast with Kant—but I had no idea how to draw out the implications of these intuitions in a constructive manner.

Students have a way of making more of a course than a teacher even knew was in it. That is certainly what Rev. Wadell has done with this wonderful book—a book that at once humbles and gladdens me. It gladdens me to see how he has imaginatively transformed the "stuff" of that course into a constructive account of the Christian moral life; it humbles me because reading this book reminds me that the work we are called to do as theologians really should make a difference for our own and other lives. Accordingly this is not just another book in moral theology, but it is a book that is meant to engage seriously and, perhaps, change our lives by helping us discover that God means to claim us as a friend through our learning to be friends with one another.

Therefore this book is not just a theoretical argument about how moral theology might be done if it took friendship more seriously, but rather the book exhibits how without friendship our lives morally are not worth living. Yet Wadell's strong argument about the importance of friendship has often been missed in Christian moral reflection because the preferential nature of friendship seems to be in tension with the Christian obligation to love all people. By locating friendship within the story of God's redemption through Christ, Wadell helps us see that the very idea we must choose between the universal or preferential friendship is based on a mistaken account of friendship. He does this by showing how friendship rightly understood cannot help but lead us to new friends without in any way denying their inherent particularity. For a friendship but names that relation in which we learn to rejoice in the particularity of the other and in the process learn how that particularity enlivens our own and other lives.

This point, moreover, accounts for the extraordinary style of this book. Wadell writes in an engaging manner drawing on novels and his own experience to illumine his position. This is not just a tactic to make the text more readable or accessible to those not trained in moral theology. Rather the stories Wadell narrates are intrinsic to his position as he must help us appreciate how the particularity of our lives are constitutive of the kind of friendship that makes friendship with God possible. But narratives require details—like drinking Virginia Dare sodas with a friend or riding F-trains to New York—that help us capture our narratives and friendships that we might otherwise fail to acknowledge. Wadell is a moral theologian with the eye of an artist, and I am convinced anyone reading this book will realize Wadell has set a new paradigm for how moral theology should be conceived.

The fact that this is a book in moral theology that is done with such style and verve may lead those who associate moral theology with more formal argument to overlook this book's considerable methodological importance. To be sure, this book can be read for profit by both laity and professional moral theologian. But it is important that those in the latter category not miss this book's extraordinary importance as a model for how moral theology might be done that avoids that unhappy distinction between spiritual and moral theology. For here is a book written in a manner that wants to make us better through the reading of it. I would like to think this at last is the kind of moral theology for which Vatican II called—that is, moral theology enriched by biblical and theological reflection. Moreover, it is distinctly Catholic, but in being so it is determinatively ecumenical. Thus in the same book we have Aquinas and Barth being used to equal effect to advance our understanding of friendship.

Another reason the systematic significance of Wadell's book for moral theology may be overlooked is that he does not write as a polemicist. He is clearly at odds with both the style and substance of Catholic moral theology, both in its conservative and liberal forms. Yet he is not out to score points against past positions or people. Rather what we find here is an attempt to do moral theology in a constructive manner that can enliven all our lives by helping us discover the telos that gives our lives more coherence. That is why this book is at once so radical and yet so conservative, for Wadell means to do nothing less than to see how our everyday lives are charged with God's grandeur.

It is equally important that the political implications of this book not be missed. Amid all the discussion about liberation theology, the social and political implications of a book like Wadell's can be overlooked. For it is Wadell's argument that a community and corresponding political organization is to be judged by its capacity to engender lives capable of forming friendships. Accounts of friendship are thus prior to accounts of justice. Therefore he joins hands with the insights of some feminists in challenging contemporary social practices that make friendship so unlikely.

This book, therefore, will not be easily characterized or pigeon-holed in terms of our contemporary disciplinary boxes or current intellectual styles. Rather it is a book of great seriousness and great humor, for what could be more serious than the joy that comes with the discovery that we are meant to be friends with God?

Finally, Wadell's book at least means, for me, that I will continue year after year to take graduate students through seminars on Aristotle, Aquinas, Kant, and Barth. I do so, not because I have got any clearer idea of what I am doing, but because Wadell's book convinces me that in spite of the teacher it can have very rich results; or, even more important, it means that through that process I discover that my students have become my teachers and hopefully my friends.

Stanley Hauerwas
The Divinity School
Duke University

Preface

This book is an argument for another way to think about the moral life. It is hard to say where it began. In one sense it began in the fall of 1981 when I started reading Aristotle and noticed friendship was integral to his conception of the moral life. But Aristotle articulated something of which I was always convinced, that friendships are not only enjoyable, they are also highly morally formative, and in this sense, long before my reading of Aristotle, the book took shape in those friendships that continue to change my life. Aristotle, along with Augustine, Aelred of Rievaulx, and Aquinas, tutored me in an insight: The moral life is the seeking of and growing in the good in the company of friends who also want to be good. Friendship is the crucible of the moral life, the relationship in which we come to embody the good by sharing it with friends who also delight in the good.

Obviously, this gives a different slant to the moral life; it nurtures a special perspective. It is not an approach to the moral life that begins by focusing on problems, for it argues that even our ability to identify a problem, much less solve it, is an implication of our character, a ·measure of our virtue. In this respect, the book fits well with the recent literature on a virtue approach to ethics, especially the writings of Stanley Hauerwas, Alasdair MacIntyre, and Gilbert C. Meilaender. In the spirit of these writers, this book argues that the central concern of the moral life is the formation of a good and worthy character, the development of virtues that will help guide us to authentic human flourishing. That is why the first part of the book gives so much attention to Aristotle.

But like Aristotle, we want to know how the virtues are acquired, we want some understanding of the kinds of contexts or relationships necessary for developing the skills requisite for wholesome living. This is where friendship emerges. Acquiring virtues takes time, they are skills honed over a lifetime. Virtues require stable, enduring relationships. But they also require good relationships. Virtues are habits we develop by practice, but we must learn what it means to practice a particular virtue and have the opportunity to grow in it through relationships with others who share our hunger for the good. Growth in virtue is not accidental; it takes place through the ongoing relationships we have with people who are one with us in what we consider important, one with us in what we most deeply desire. These people are our best and closest friends, and because what we desire matters to them as well, it is with and through them that our moral development primarily occurs.

A second characteristic of this approach to the moral life is that it emphasizes and insists on the relational quality of our lives. It does not fit in the Kantian tradition; it does not see moral agents as isolated, solitary individuals who must make choices and decisions by stepping back from their world, by abstracting from their histories, by denying all those things that make them who they are. In this respect, the book fits well with the literature of recent feminist ethics. It appeals to our experience; it asks us to reflect on how so much of who we are is the work of friends who love us and suggests that the moral life is not something that occurs when we step outside those friendships, but is precisely the ongoing life of the friendships themselves.

For a long time I have felt that many contemporary approaches to the moral life were too narrow, too tightly construed; clarity was gained at the cost of richness. There was precision, but large areas of life were left untouched. This is not to deny that models for the moral life that focus on problem solving are important, but it is to say if that becomes the dominant paradigm for ethics, then our sense of morality is severely impoverished. If morality concerns the most personal things about us, then it must concern us as persons in all the levels and dimensions of our lives. It must risk taking us as a whole, it must ask about what we love, about our deepest concerns, about the people whose love for us is something from which we never recover. This makes ethics messier, but far more interesting and eminently more practical because it makes it an investigation of how we actually practice our lives. Decisions are important in the moral life, but major decisions, hopefully, are relatively few. What matters most is what happens between the times of those decisions. How are we being formed? What do our loves make of us? What is happening to our character?

This book is an invitation to open up our sense of the moral life. It begins with an appeal to our experience. The first chapter starts with a lengthy recollection of formative friendships in my own life. If friendship is a suitable model for the moral life, then it is one that sees morality as a way of life pursued in the ongoing history of special relationships; this is why the book begins not in abstract reflection, but in the concreteness of particular friendships. It begins with a story not only because stories are usually interesting, but because it argues that if friendship is our model for ethics, then the moral life is the saga of the most formative and enriching relationships of our lives. In the first chapter we examine the implications of some contemporary approaches to ethics, and in light of them suggest why friendship may be a promising way to think about morality. The chapter concludes with the suggestion that the moral life is not primarily a matter of decisions and problem solving, but of making good on the purpose in which happiness and wholeness consists. It is a matter of discovering what counts for the best of lives, of knowing what it is a human being should try to become if one's life is not to be wasted. Friendship is essential here because we have access to the goods that bring us to fullness only in company with those who share them.

Chapter two begins our study of Aristotle. Aristotle understood the moral life to be clustered around a specific reckoning of the purpose of being human and the virtues necessary to achieve it. Friendship was an intrinsic good in Aristotle's schema of ethics, but largely because it was the relationship in which people could come to understand and participate in the purpose for which life is given. They did this through acquiring and practicing the virtues. In this respect, friendship functions as the fundamental life activity in which men and women live now, however incompletely, the wholeness human life is given to achieve. The third chapter continues this study of Aristotle by considering how Aristotle understood friendship, how he delineated different kinds of friendships, and why, for him, we need them to become good.

The fourth chapter takes up a different theme. In much of the Christian tradition friendship has been suspect because it is a preferential love. In contrast, Christian love or agape is seen to be universal and inclusive. Given this description, friendship could hardly count as Christian love; at worst it was totally inimical to Christian love, at best a necessary preparation for Christian love. If friendship is to be a model for the moral life, this challenge from the Christian tradition must be addressed. In this chapter we examine the writings of Soren Kierkegaard and Anders Nygren, both of whom saw Christian love as a rejection of friendship. In response, we explore the thought of Augustine, Aelred of Rievaulx, and Karl Barth. What we learn from this comparison is that whether friendship is at odds with Christian love depends on one's narrative account of friendship. If it is a friendship centered in Christ, then far from being a love agape leaves behind, Christian friendships are those in which the friends learn to love all those God loves. In short, agape describes the ever widening scope of a friendship whose members are trying to be like God.

Thomas Aquinas said charity is a "certain friendship" men and women are called to have with God. For Thomas, charity is not only a single virtue, but a comprehensive description of what he took the fullness of life to be. To be human is to seek and enjoy friendship with God, a friendship which begins in this world by grace, is strengthened through the virtues, and is brought to perfection by the Spirit. Chapter five looks at Thomas's understanding of charity as friendship with God. It considers why Thomas can make such an astonishing claim, and why he insists it is in something so fabulous that fullness resides. The chapter concludes with a discussion of Thomas's analysis of the three marks of friendship and what this means when the friend in mind is God.

The book closes with a chapter investigating how friendship as a model for the moral life might work in everyday life. It talks about a stance of hospitality or openness to others so that those who might now be strangers to us can become our friends. It asks us to consider how so much of the moral life for us turns on whether we are able to see others as blessings and gifts instead of threats to be feared. More than anything, this final chapter studies what good and lasting friendships do to us, how they shape our sense of self, how they enable identity and respect, how another's wanting what is best for us empowers us to seek friendships with others. Put differently, if friendship is an integral element to a flourishing life, this chapter discloses what a serious moral problem it is to be without good friends.

It is good friends who have helped see this book to completion. Special thanks must be given to Stanley Hauerwas, Charlie Pinches, and Philip Foubert for encouraging me to develop these ideas on friendship. It was Stanley Hauerwas especially, my mentor at the University of Notre Dame, who supported my enthusiasm for this project. I must also thank John Ehmann of the University of Notre Dame Press for his thoughtful suggestions and kind support, Carole Roos for her help in editing, and Kenneth O'Malley, C.P., and Marylyn Welter, S.S.S.F., for their work in preparing the text.

I have worked on this project while teaching Christian ethics at Catholic Theological Union in Chicago. It is a splendid atmosphere for teaching and writing, and I am grateful for the friendship and support of its faculty.

Finally, this book begins with stories of friendship in my earliest years with the Passionist Community. It is my brothers in community who have taught me so richly the preciousness of good friendships, who have tutored me in its graces, who have strengthened me in its hopes. Living with them has always been what Aelred of Rievaulx said good friendships should be, people thriving together in Christ. Their friendship is the inspiration for this book, so to them I am especially grateful.

1. Friendship and the Moral Life:

Why a New Model for Morality Is Needed

I. An Autobiographical Beginning

In the fall of 1965 two hundred of us embarked on an adventure from which we never fully recovered. We left our homes in Saint Louis, Chicago, Detroit, California, Louisville—others from places remembered only by them—and journeyed to a little town in eastern Missouri called Warrenton, to a high school seminary called Mother of Good Counsel, to a religious community called the Passionists, to a large rambling pink stucco building that never quite fit the landscape but for the next four years would be our home.

Life was different, people were happy—that is the first thing we noticed about Warrenton and what we always remember. What made it different and its memory lasting was what the school was trying to achieve. At Warrenton, they were not just trying to teach us, they were also trying to change us, to form and shape us, to take us as we were, all raw, unfinished youth, and make us something more. Warrenton was an experiment, a dream perhaps, born from the conviction that life has a purpose and our happiness is achieving it. There was the deep belief that all of us have to become more than we already are, we have to change, we have to become as good as we possibly can. It is never enough just to be ourselves, we have to grow, to be transfigured from sinners into friends of God. Warrenton was

1

not just a school, it was a way of life, a vision that made the everyday a grammar for our hopes, and because we shared the same hopes we were able to become good friends.

The most remarkable fact about Warrenton was that all of us who came there strangers left there friends. On a Saturday in May 1969, lives so unexpectedly brought together were just as unexpectedly torn apart. We left to different futures—most to marriage, a few to religious life and priesthood, some to futures never revealed to the rest of us—but we left as friends. Even though we did not understand then what those friendships meant to us, nor how deeply and poignantly we had touched each other's lives, it is a tribute to those friendships that so many years later when we hear the word "friend" it is each other we remember.

Warrenton was a school of friendship. That was its most remarkable achievement, its enduring legacy. But it was not its explicit purpose. We went there not to be friends but to discover if we ought to be Passionists. Scattered all across the country, people of different backgrounds, talents, personalities and temperaments did something very odd in 1965: In answer to an inkling, we left our homes, journeyed to the rural Missouri countryside (an unlikely place to augur the future), and for the next four years pledged to see life with people we had never met. It was a strange scenario, two hundred boys on the threshold of adolescence, each a parable of all the turns a life can take, inducted into a world established to fathom a promise. It was not a world that would make sense to most, all its strange practices, its baffling rules, but it was a world that could make a single possibility real, and in whatever measure we gave ourselves to that we found a memory from which hope continues to be born.

A few days before Christmas 1968 several of us gathered for Eucharist. It was evening, it was cold, it was peaceful. We stood in a circle around a small table which served as the altar, our faces shadowy, illumined only by the soft glow of Christmas lights scattered throughout the room. Something happened during that Eucharist; we found another reason for giving thanks. As we stood there and looked at one another we realized, perhaps for the first time, that we were indebted. We realized how much we had shaped and formed one another through an odyssey of four years, and, almost to our surprise, how close we had become, how fused our lives had grown. In that Eucharist we realized here were people we loved. It was a revelation to realize the intimacy that lived among us. Its discovery was almost a shock, because we had not set forth four years before to become friends, we had set forth to explore an intuition, to discern a grace, and now we faced an ending that took us by surprise, for though very few of us ended up Passionists, all of us ended up friends. That evening in Eucharist we encircled another offer of friendship. We closed in on a God we can hold in our hands, and as we picked that God up, placed Him in our mouths, and prayed that He would enter our hearts, we sensed for an instant why people we might never see again were people we would never forget. As God melted away in us, a memory formed within.

It is always that way with friendships; we do not aim for them directly, we discover them. Friendships are not sought, they emerge. They take shape among people of shared purpose, they grow from the soil of similar interests and concerns. Warrenton was a school of friendship not because it sought to make us friends, but because it presented us with a purpose that made friendship possible. The intimacy we felt that night in Eucharist, and the transition from strangeness to kinship it marked, would never have occurred if we had not assented to a way of life designed to uncover whether that promise was ours. One of the mysteries of Warrenton was that for most of us it was not, one of the graces of Warrenton was that the discipline required for that discovery blessed us with an intimacy that so many years later still feels amazingly fresh.

Warrenton presented us with an adventure worthy of ourselves. To become part of that adventure, to say yes to a story that from without looked so very odd, such a strange way to navigate adolescence, was from within the grandest of joys, for it taught us that our happiness lay not in the unimpeded extolling of our freedom, but in the mutual, communal submission of our lives to a purpose. In short, we were friends not because we first liked each other, but because together we pursued a way of life which formed us in the very things we came to discover we loved. It was this intuitive, seldom articulated, consensus on what we took to be the project and purpose of our life that made us such good friends and allowed our differences to contribute to a unity we otherwise never would have found. Those friendships formed twenty years ago are amazingly resilient, not because there was anything particularly special about the participants, but because there was something noble about the adventure.

Books on the moral life do not usually begin with musings from one's adolescence; however, those musings embody an argument about another, hopefully compelling, way to consider the moral life. Warrenton was not just a school, it was a moral argument. It was an experiment in a very specific understanding of how we ought to live, and to consider it now is not to wax nostalgic on the merits of an era that will never be retrieved, but to suggest such an understanding of life has to be recovered if we are to fathom and appreciate what we mean when we describe our life as moral. Too often we narrow the focus of morality to decisions we occasionally make or problems that periodically confront us; however, the scope of morality is much grander and more dramatic than that. Morality is the arena in which persons are made or broken, in which lives succeed or are wasted. What this language suggests is that being human is a matter of doing something definitive. To be human is to have a purpose to fulfill, a goal into which we must grow, and we cannot be indifferent to this purpose, for to neglect it is to fail as a human being.

The genius of Warrenton is that it recognized morality as a question of making a single possibility real. This way of life was exactly what was required for being transformed into a person whose life gave glory to God. Warrenton was an argument which said to be human was to have a story to live and the task of our lifetime is to live so that we not only bring that story to completion, but come to embody the fullness the story represents. In Christian language, to be human is to grow to our fullness in Christ, to make good on the singular possibility of becoming as much like God as we possibly can. Such a possibility is not one option among others in the human adventure, it is its very soul. And the Christian life is precisely the discipline—the collection of practices and activities and habits—which enables the realization of this single possibility.

What Warrenton also represented as an argument for the moral life is not only that when we pursue these possibilities we discover friendships with others who share them, but that we need friends to realize these possibilities at all. Friendships come to be through goals that are shared, through common interests and concerns, but those very goals that entice us come to be only through the friendships they create. Morality involves the pursuit and achievement of some good, but that pursuit and achievement requires friendship, the ongoing presence of another who not only shares that good, but in relationship with whom the good can be received. Morality is the pursuit of a good capable of making us whole, but morality is possible only because there are others, and that is one reason friendship is so delightful, it puts goodness within our reach.

Thus, friendship is not just a good for the moral life, it is indispensable; there simply is no other way to come in touch with the goods that make us whole than through relationships with those who share them. That is why we can say friendship is the crucible of moral development, the center of moral formation. One reason we have friends is that there is a good we share with them, but the reason friendships grow and become such a delight is that we cannot be good without them, indeed, we cannot be at all. On this account, it shall not be surprising that we can speak of marriage as a kind of friendship, or of religious life as a community of friends, or even of the church as all those joined through friendship in Christ.

On a Saturday early in March when the first touches of a luscious Missouri spring could be felt in the air, a classmate walked me out the front gate of the seminary down Highway M into Warrenton. Our destination was the IGA Foodstore. My friend took out a quarter, plopped it into a machine, and pulled out a bottle of Virginia Dare Creme Soda. We went outside, sat down on the curb, and in the perfect sunlight of that Saturday watched the cars roll by. We sat for a long time, saying little. We watched the procession of pickup trucks and tractors, but we were thinking of something else. In less than three months our adventure would be over, we would be pulled apart to futures we could only dimly see, and this frightened us. But we were also thinking about how over the stretch of four years two very different characters, one from Saint Louis, the other from Louisville, had each become the other's gift, teasing out possibilities neither could have realized alone. We were thinking of the good times we had shared, of the crazy pranks we plotted, but more than anything we were feeling grateful, indebted, unusually appreciative of one without whom we could not have been ourselves. We sat there for a long time because it was a moment we did not want to pass. We wanted to savor it, to offer it up in some kind of thanksgiving, for near the end of our shared adventure we had come to see we were different than we had been when the adventure began. We had changed, we had grown, and even though we would soon be walking into a future we could hardly predict, we had that afternoon, over a bottle of Virginia Dare Creme Soda, found a memory strong enough to guide us in hope.

The moral life is often such retrospective activity because sooner or later we try to understand what has made us who we are. This leads us to certain people. We remember them, we cherish them, we are grateful to them because we realize we could not have been ourselves without them. We call these people friends, whether they be our parents, our sisters and brothers, childhood companions, or even strangers whose moment of kindness came at an hour of need. When we think of the moral life, it is not surprising we think of them. They taught us the good. They formed us. Through their love they chiseled in us qualities we could not have reached alone. When we think of the moral life, we do not remember only the decisions we sometimes had to make, even the problems that may have beset us, we also remember our friends and the life that was shared between us. There seemed to be nothing better than to be with them, that somehow being with them was being ourself, that somehow who we were was exactly the friendships that meant so much to us. When we think of the moral life we remember these friendships because intuitively we sense it is whatever happened in them that helped us grow good. In so many respects, morality is what happens between friends. It is not the whole of the moral life, but there can be no moral life without it.

Friendship is an appealing model for the moral life, but why? Perhaps because it honors our experience. Few of us have gone through high school seminaries, but all of us have been friends. So much of our life *is* a history of our friendships. Still, we are not accustomed to think of the moral life as friendship—we are not even accustomed to think about friendship as moral. But maybe we should. If so much of who we are is the handiwork of our friends, and if the good in which we need to be transfigured is one we do not grasp for but receive in relationships with others, then we need to give careful attention to how friendships figure in the moral life.

The moral life is the formation of people in the good in relationships with people who are good. This is what it means to speak of the moral life as friendship. And even though it may strike us as a novel idea, it is one with a venerable, if forgotten, heritage. Both Aristotle and Saint Thomas Aquinas described the moral life in terms of friendship. Like all great moralists, Aristotle and Aquinas struggled to understand how we are to make our lives as a whole. What ought we to do with ourselves? How do we end up with a life that is both happy and good? What must become of us, how must we live, act, and behave, if our life at its end is not to be judged a failure? They answered this question in different ways, but both answered it through friendship. They understood morality to be the task of becoming a certain kind of person, of growth according to a good, but they spoke of this in the language of friendship because they suspected it was in the context of friendship that the virtues which make us whole would be learned.

The argument of this book is the same. The moral life involves the transformation of the self according to a good which represents human fullness, but that transformation occurs in the embrace of relationships with others who share our love. Before we consider what friendship means for the moral life, we need to examine what our sense of morality may be now. What are some characteristics of contemporary morality? What is our sense of it? As we look across our moral landscape, what do we see? How we answer these questions may help us appreciate the rationale for friendship as a model for the moral life; indeed, it may be that the inadequacy of our sense of the moral life is what makes the notion of friendship so enticing.

II. Why a New Model for the Moral Life Is Needed

One day, a few weeks before I began teaching my first class, I was down in the lobby of the school fetching my mail. A young man standing nearby told me he was registered for my introductory course in ethics to begin that spring. When you first begin teaching you are not sure if anyone is going to take your class, so this bit of news was welcome. I responded that I was happy to hear this and looked forward to having him in class. Then, without a second's hesitation, the student looked at me and said, "Well, I hate ethics."

I did not know whether to admire him for his courage or be nonplussed by his nerve, but I remember that little incident often for I suspect he captures how many of us feel about morality. We may not go so far as to say we "hate ethics," but the thought of contemporary morality likely leaves us uneasy. Consider how we feel when moral topics are introduced. We grow anxious, we have a sense that these discussions will drag on, resolving nothing, leaving people angry and divided. We remember similar moments when we walked away weary but not enlightened, not just because the conversation seemed interminable, but because it left us feeling isolated in the company of our own principles and values. We grow uneasy when people start to talk about ethics, not because ethical discussions are always complex, but because they are so often divisive, sad reminders of how far apart we are on things we consider important.

Moral discussion distresses us because it often confirms what we have come to suspect but hate to acknowledge: a loss of confidence in morality's point and purpose. What unsettles us is that something which ought to help us see more clearly the point and purpose of our life is in disarray. And it is not just the fact of disagreement that concerns us, for conflict has always been part of morality, but that disagreement prevails. Instead of sharpening our awareness of what the good life demands, it reminds us that the notion of the good life has been forgotten. [1]

Ambivalence may best describe our feelings towards morality. On the one hand, we say, and we intuitively sense, that ethics has to do with the deepest values and concerns of our life. It has to do with what we love and cherish, with our dreams and our hopes, with all those things to which we are devoted. Intuitively we know that ethics is not primarily a matter of rules and principles, of duties and obligations, of laws pushed down on us from without, for none of these is intelligible apart from the goods we cannot afford to lose; rather, it is a scrutiny of all those things to which we must learn to be devoted if we are to find peace. Morality, we sense, is not something apart from us, it is the most personal thing about us. It is an attempt to understand what we should do with the precious lifetime we have been given.

How must our life be shaped? What must become of us if we are to be both happy and good? That question unveils the substance of morality for it takes our life as a whole and focuses on morality's preeminent concern: How ought we to live? In his book, *Ethics and the Limits of Philosophy,* Bernard Williams notes that this is the question with which Socrates began, and it is "the best place for moral philosophy to start." [2] The value of this question is that it extends the vista of morality beyond the everyday, it enlarges the vision of our concerns beyond the immediate into the future. As Williams puts it, Socrates' question stretches our perspective of the moral life because it does not ask 'what shall I do,' but 'how shall I live.' "This is one way in which Socrates' question goes beyond the everyday," he says. "Another is that it is not immediate; it is not about what I should do now, or next. It is about a manner of life. The Greeks themselves were much impressed by the idea that such a question must, consequently, be about a whole life and that a good way of living had to issue in what, at its end, would be seen to have been a good life." [3]

The Second Vatican Council took the same approach. It is often noted that the Council said little explicitly about Catholic moral theology, but what it did say was important. In *Optatan Totius,* the *Decree on the Training of Priests,* the Council exhorted Catholic moral theologians to renew moral theology by focusing it on Christ and our vocation in Christ as the principle and center of the Catholic moral life. "Special care," the Council said, "should be given to the perfecting of moral theology. Its scientific presentation should draw more fully on the teaching of holy Scripture and should throw light upon the exalted vocation of the faithful in Christ and their obligation to bring forth fruit in charity for the life of the world."[4]

That is Socrates' question in a new key. The Council poses the question of how we should take our life as a whole. What must happen in the course of our lifetime if that life is not to be judged a failure? And from the perspective of Christian faith they answer we must grow to our fullness in Christ. The Council tried to move Catholic morality away from an approach that was overly juridical and that too often focused on evil to be avoided rather than on good to be done. The reason for that shift was based in the conviction that the fullness of the good life is seen in Christ, that we do what we ought to do when we become as much like God as we possibly can through a discipleship life with Christ. Though this single paragraph comprises a very small part of the *Council Documents,* what it says is explosive, for it challenges Catholic moralists to reformulate their whole understanding of the moral life. If the preeminent moral question, as Williams suggested, is not 'what should we do now?' but 'what should we become?' then the Council suggests we should become godly. We should submit to that transfiguration unto holiness that the odyssey of discipleship entails.

These are sweeping moral questions, but they remind us that morality is not something other than our life, but is an explicit articulation of what our life entails. Socrates answered it one way, the Council another, but both suggest morality concerns the comprehensive arena of our life. It concerns us not piecemeal but entire, with a strategy not only to direct our behavior but to change our hearts. It is a vision of the moral life we seldom encounter in the literature of ethics today precisely because it is so complete. It is sweeping, it is daring, it pointedly declares that being human means making good on a promise, that it means making some single possibility real, and for the Council, that single possibility is fulsome life with God mediated through discipleship life with Christ.

This compelling vision sets the stakes of the moral life high, yet it is a vision we seldom associate with morality today. Intuitively we sense that morality deals with the deepest concerns and values of our life, that its scope is our grandest possibilities, and if we are Christian we connect these possibilities to Christ; yet, when we turn to ethics these dimensions seem to be missing. This is the core irony nestled deep in contemporary ethics. Intuitively we sense what the moral life involves, but when we turn to literature on ethics these concerns are seldom discussed; thus, ethics fails us at the point it should help us most. It fails its most basic function of helping us see more clearly what we should take our life to be and what we should try to achieve.

When we survey the literature today what we too often discover is not something to guide and instruct us, but an approach that does not go deep enough. What is missing is any normative sense of what being human entails. This is why we feel ethics so often misses the mark. We know morality involves becoming a certain kind of person. We know it entails a transformation of self through habits and practices that work changes necessary for goodness. As Christians, we know the moral life is the spiritual life, the religious-sacramental life we have with God, a studied, ongoing attempt to establish ourselves God's friends. We find ourselves nodding in agreement with the whisky-priest in Graham Greene's great novel, *The Power and the Glory,* who shortly before his death, "felt like someone who has missed happiness by seconds at an appointed place. He knew now that at the end there was only one thing that counted—to be a saint."[5] That is a compelling insight that prompts us to consider our life in a new key. What if it is so that "at the end" there is only one thing that counts, to be a saint? How then should we live?

What confounds us about morality today is that too often it fails to address the very questions about which we should be most concerned. It is not nervy enough. We want to be good, but there is little assurance of what it means to be good. We want to make something of ourselves, we do not want to come up short; but we have few clear reasons which suggest exactly what this change should be. These lifetime questions are quintessentially moral, but they are too infrequently posed. We need a magnanimous ethic, which is perfecting precisely because it aspires to greatness. "Magnanimity," Josef Pieper says, "decides in favor of what is, at any given moment, the greater possibility of the human potentiality for being,"[6] and that is a moral life worthy of ourselves. Morality today does not ask enough of us. It is complex, it is technical, it is sophisticated, but it is not always costly. It is costly to say our life means putting on Christ and growing to our fullness in Christ, but at least that offers us an adventure worthy of ourself and promises a transformation that is stunning.

We need morality to guide us in our appreciation of the good and in fostering the right kind of desires. We need it to assist us in cultivating the proper kinds of loves, in developing attachments that will not destroy us. We want a risky, magnanimous ethics, and we are disenchanted when ethics takes silence as its response. Our uneasiness with contemporary morality does not signal disinterest but disappointment.

Stanley Hauerwas is one contemporary ethicist who has raised these points. In his book, *The Peaceable Kingdom*, Hauerwas remarks that the most common sentiment associated with ethics today is anxiety. He considers this odd. Morality ought to challenge us, but it should also reassure us. It ought to critique our lives, but it should also help us sustain them. Indeed, even though morality ought to call us to conversion, it should make us enthusiastic about what that conversion promises. Morality ought to evoke many sentiments, but it is strange, Hauerwas argues, that anxiety would be primary. Why is this so? Hauerwas answers that the primary moral questions have become the burden of the individual to answer. We are left to ourselves to determine what the moral life means, to delineate its point and purpose, and while this undoubtedly gives us a sense of freedom, and perhaps even a sense of power, it also makes us anxious. If the crucial moral questions admit only of individual answers, the most meaningful convictions of our life are haunted by an awful arbitrariness.

There is a terrible loneliness in this kind of freedom. It forces us to suppress those things we feel most deeply about exactly because the only warrant we have for holding them is that they happen to be our own. We are reluctant to unveil what we believe because we are hard pressed to explain why our beliefs might have merit for anyone other than ourself. Consequently, those things about which we care the most are also the things about which we are most silent. We carry the moral life quietly, buried deep, isolated by the fear that what is precious to us is only what we prefer. Ironically, the freedom we are given to determine the moral life for ourselves becomes a burden which grows heavier with each step. Not surprisingly, in this approach to the moral life, friendship is seldom discussed. As Hauerwas comments,

> This lurking suspicion that we really have no firm grounds for our beliefs makes us all the more unwilling to expose what we think to critical scrutiny. We thus take refuge among others who think as we do, hoping sheer numbers will protect us from the knowledge of our uncertainty. Or sometimes we

suppose that if we think deeply and critically about our moral convictions, we will be able to supply adequate justification for what we believe. In both cases we assume that "ethics" must be able to provide the means for preventing our world from falling into a deeper moral chaos.

Underlying such a view of morality is the presupposition that we are required by our modern predicament to make up our "own minds" about what is good and bad. Indeed, those who do so with determination are seen as morally exemplary because they act autonomously rather than uncritically accept convention. But the very notion we are "choosing" or "making up" our morality contains the seeds of its own destruction, for moral authenticity seems to require that morality be not a matter of one's own shaping, but something that shapes one. We do not create moral values, principles, virtues; rather they constitute a life for us to appropriate. The very idea that we choose what is valuable undermines our confidence in its worth.[7]

Hauerwas's closing comment that "moral authenticity seems to require that morality be not a matter of one's own shaping, but something that shapes one," and that "we do not create moral values, principles, virtues; rather they constitute a life for us to appropriate," is telling because it repositions us toward the moral life. It inverts our perspective on morality because suddenly we see that morality is not something we create, but something by which we are claimed. If this becomes the principle from which we consider the moral life, our understanding of its constitutive elements alters drastically. The emphasis now is not so much on the freedom to choose, but the freedom to be faithful to a way of life. The emphasis now is not on values we create, but on values we discover, goods to which we submit precisely because moral wholeness is not a matter of autonomy but of *ascesis,* the participation of the self in a way of life whose virtues and practices can work the transformation necessary for wholeness. Once we view the moral life as an assignment to carry out, our sense of it is different. It cannot be anything we want, it cannot adequately be described as what we decide to do with our freedom; but something we discover and to which we are to be faithful.

We need a model for morality that emphasizes fidelity more than freedom, transformation more than choice. We need a model which reminds us that the moral life is the disciplined, skilled endeavor to conform ourselves to the purposes in which fullness of life consists. The danger with much of our moral thinking is that it lures us into believing the moral world is no bigger than ourselves, thus it is nothing other than what we in our freedom make of it. The philosopher-novelist Iris Murdoch speaks of this in her essay, "Against Dryness: A Polemical Sketch." She claims much of our contemporary moral thinking is influenced by the Kantian view that each individual "is rational and totally free. . . . He is morally speaking monarch of all he surveys and totally responsible for his actions. Nothing transcends him. His moral language is a practical pointer, the instrument of his choices, the indication of his preferences."[8] If each person is "monarch" of all he or she surveys, they in their freedom become the arbiters of the moral world—they stand as the single principle in reference to which everything else gets its meaning. As Murdoch explains, "We no longer see man against a background of values, of realities which transcend him. We picture man as a brave naked will surrounded by an easily comprehended empirical world. For the hard idea of truth we have substituted a facile idea of sincerity."[9]

Sincerity is a very modern virtue. If there is no moral order other than what we in our freedom determine it to be, morality is a matter of preferences, and when it comes to preferences, the best one can do is be sincere. There is no truth to violate, no moral order to respect. If we are "monarchs" of all we survey, this means everything's value is a measure of what we in our freedom decide. As the authors of *Habits of the Heart,* the gripping study of what

Americans think about happiness, freedom, and commitment, put it, "Now if selves are defined by their preferences, but those preferences are arbitrary, then each self constitutes its own moral universe, and there is finally no way to reconcile conflicting claims about what is good in itself."[10]

Thus, freedom becomes both more important than goodness and independent of goodness. On this view, morality has no meaning, even no reality, apart from what we determine. The moral life is not a seeking of the true and the good, because there is neither truth nor goodness apart from ourselves. Each individual is the source of her or his moral universe. Morality is created anew through the exercise of freedom—it is we who bring it into being—because goodness does not preexist freedom as something freedom should serve, but freedom preexists goodness as the power necessary to determine what goodness will be. Values have no reality outside of the choices we make. However, while it is enticing to think we create the moral world, ultimately it is disturbing, because it means there is no necessary connection between how we decide, choose, and act, and reality. This is a dangerous illusion for it kills the wonder which makes us ask if there might be a world larger than ourselves with a purpose to which we must conform. As Murdoch summarizes,

> A simpleminded faith in science, together with the assumption that we are all rational and totally free, engenders a dangerous lack of curiosity about the real world, a failure to appreciate the difficulties of knowing it. We need to return from the self-centered concept of sincerity to the other-centered concept of truth. We are not isolated free choosers, monarchs of all we survey, but benighted creatures sunk in a reality whose nature we are constantly and overwhelmingly tempted to deform by fantasy."[11]

The moral life is placing ourself in relationship to a good we lack but need to possess if our life is not to be wasted.

We only see this when we realize the moral world is much larger and infinitely more compelling than what we in our freedom could ever make it to be. We only see this when we come to realize there is something independent of our freedom and preferences that we must come to know, love, and serve, a goodness in whose likeness we must be transformed if our life is not to be a loss. That is strong, disturbing language, but morality is serious business; what hangs in the balance is the outcome of our life.

A second reason we may have ambivalent feelings towards morality is that many of us do not think of our life as moral until we are in some kind of a mess. Think of it. Is it not true that the experiences to which we give the name moral are usually troublesome situations in which we find ourselves and are not sure how to respond? If someone were to play a word association game and tossed out the word 'moral', what would first come to mind? For many of us it would not be our dreams and aspirations, projects and purposes, not even our loves; no, likely it would be regrettable instances we are not sure how we entered and have little idea how to escape. On this view, we do not think of our lives as moral, we think of our problems as moral. This perspective might be implicit, but it is pervasive.

Instead of seeing morality positively as the ongoing pursuit of the good, we cast it in negative terms, limiting its relevance to situations which confound us. Edmund Pincoffs calls this 'quandary ethics'. It is the view that morality operates in times of crisis, that its chief business is the solving of problems. In quandary ethics, Pincoffs says, the focus of morality is not our life as a whole, but the difficult situations we sometimes face but are not sure how to resolve. As Pincoffs writes,

> There is a consensus concerning the subject-matter of ethics so general that it would be tedious to document it. It is that the business of ethics is with "problems," that is, situations in which it is difficult to know what one should do; that the

ultimate beneficiary of ethical analysis is the person who, in one of these situations, seeks rational ground for the decision he must make; that ethics is therefore primarily concerned to find such grounds, often conceived of as moral rules and the principles from which they can be derived; and that meta-ethics consists in the analysis of the terms, claims, and arguments which come into play in moral disputation, deliberation, and justification in problematic concepts.[12]

In quandary ethics, morality operates in times of crisis, but if this is so, how can we ever come to embrace it? It is true that one of the functions of ethics is to help us act when we are not sure how to act, but if morality is exclusively this, or even primarily this, it leaves so much of our life untouched. In short, if we notice morality only when we have problems, there is so much we do not notice at all. Pincoffs does not deny that sometimes we face difficult problems and it is the business of ethics to address these, but he does deny that this is all ethics does. The 'problem' with quandary ethics is that even when it helps us, it remains essentially apart from us, something which enters our life from the outside when we need to be rescued from situations we cannot understand. It is not seen as something integral to life, but persists as something to which we are essentially at odds. Sometimes we are confounded by problems for which there are no easy answers, and in these moments we need the guidance, the collective wisdom of others; however, if ethics remains a sign that something in our life has gone wrong instead of a description of what our life as a whole is about, then even when it serves us it signals something we would rather avoid. In quandary ethics, morality has the status of intruder, it matters most when somehow our life is not what it should be.

There is a further twist to this. By making problems and not persons the principal focus of ethics, we forget that the problems we confront and how we confront them depend on the kind of persons we have become. By reducing the scope of ethics from persons to problems, quandary ethics not only limits morality's relevance to a single dimension of our life, but forgets that the situations in which we find ourselves and how we respond to them are an implication of our character. Quandary ethics overlooks the connection between who we are and what we do. It isolates problematic moral situations as if they had a meaning apart from the people who face them. As Stanley Hauerwas comments, "'Situations' are not 'out there' waiting to be seen but are created by the kind of people we are."[13] Each of us is occasionally beset with problems, and morality should come to our assistance, but, as Hauerwas suggests, if the primary function of morality is problem solving and not persons, we never see the connection between the situations in which we find ourselves and the people we have become. We forget that how we approach a problem, even what we consider to be a problem, is largely a measure of our character; in fact, the capacity to recognize a problem is a moral skill. "The kind of quandaries we confront," Hauerwas writes, "depends on the kind of people we are and the way we have learned to construe the world through our language, habits, and feelings."[14]

Hauerwas gives the example of abortion. He notes that "the question of what I ought to do is actually about what I am or ought to be. 'Should I or should I not have an abortion?' is not just a question about an 'act' but about what kind of person I am going to be."[15] We do not all come to the same conclusion about the same situation because we are not all the same kind of person. Each of us can be confronted with the same situation, but how we read that situation, the moral assessment we give it, varies considerably in virtue of who we are. That is Hauerwas's point. We cannot separate quandaries from the persons who confront them, for we do not stand before problems as neutral spectators, but as people whose point of view is entailed by our convictions and beliefs, people whose very way of life, whose moral history, leads us to see situations a certain way. There is then an indissoluble connection between the problems we face and the people we are, a connection so tight, Hauerwas suggests, that to change our minds about a moral question is also to change ourselves. For instance, if as Christians we come to a different moral assessment of abortion, "we must recognize," Hauerwas says, "that we have not simply changed our minds about a particular act called abortion, but by changing our understanding or eliminating our notion of abortion we have in fact changed ourselves."[16]

Instead of quandary ethics, Hauerwas proposes virtue ethics. An ethic of virtue does not minimize the decisions we must sometimes make, but "refuses to make such decisions the paradigmatic center of moral reflection." An ethic of virtue sees all the decisions we make in terms of the kind of person we are. It stresses, Hauerwas says, that "morality is not primarily concerned with quandaries or hard decisions; nor is the moral self simply the collection of such decisions. As persons of character we do not confront situations as mud puddles into which we have to step; rather the kind of 'situations' we confront and how we understand them are a function of the kind of people we are." In this way, he concludes, "'training in virtue' often requires that we struggle with the moral situations which we have 'got ourselves into' in the hope that such a struggle will help us develop a character sufficient to avoid, or understand differently, such situations in the future."[17]

Quandary ethics clusters moral reflection around the question, "What should I do?" It is a key moral concern, but an ethic of virtue argues it is not an intelligible question apart from the prior and more fundamental inquiry, "Who should I become?" Quandary ethics puts the wrong question first. Edmund Pincoffs stresses that moral assessment involves not only taking into account the situation, but also the notion of "what is worthy of me: What may I permit myself to do or suffer in the light of the conception I have of my own so far formed, and still forming, moral character?"[18] Pincoffs explains that whereas quandary ethics supposes that moral assessment can be given "without any reference to me as an individual, including my personal conceptions of what are and are not worthy deeds and attitudes and feelings: worthy of me," character or virtue ethics argues that "reference to my standards and ideals is an essential, not an accidental feature of my moral deliberation. An act is or is not right from my standpoint, which is where I stand when I deliberate," he explains, "not merely as it meets or fails to meet the requirements of an ideal universal legislation, but also as it meets or fails to meet the standards I set for myself."[19]

This is putting into different language Aquinas's insight that actions cannot be understood apart from the agents who perform them, and it helps us see how we determine our moral responsibility in particular situations is largely entailed by the kind of people we are. Once we separate the decisions we must make from the person we are trying to become, we have no firm grounds for deciding one way over another. The situation becomes amazingly complex and can easily overwhelm us, not because it is necessarily complex, but because we have forsaken the identity, the moral history, which enables us to decide well at all. As long as that secondary question, "What should I do?" remains primary, not only shall we have little confidence in the decisions we make, we shall also feel at odds with the moral life. Our very understanding of it will have estranged us from what morality genuinely involves. As a result, the problems we face may well be more a reflection of a false understanding of the moral life than a particularly uncooperative world.

This association of ethics with problems has not always been the case; in fact, it is a peculiarly modern phenomenon. Pincoffs observes that "Quandary Ethics is a newcomer: that the quandarist is fighting a very long tradition with which he is at odds. Plato, Aristotle, the Epicureans, the Stoics, Augustine, Aquinas, Shaftesbury, Hume, and

Hegel do not conceive of ethics as the quandarists do." Each of these understood ethics to be "not so much concerned with problematic situations as with moral enlightenment, education, and the good for man."[20] With Aristotle, for example, ethics concerned "a very wide-ranging subject having to do generally with the planning of human life so that it could be lived as well as possible."[21] Its pressing interest was not the problems human beings face, but "the best kind of individual life, and the qualities of character exhibited by the man who leads it. . . . Moral problems are given their due but are by no means stage-center. The question is not so much how we should resolve perplexities as how we should live."[22] Thus, Pincoffs concludes, "That the moral philosopher can be thought of as prescribing a regimen for a healthy moral life rather than a cure for particular moral illnesses would surely not be news to Aristotle."[23]

Maybe that is what is called for today and what might make friendship so promising a model for the moral life. If we feel ambivalent towards morality, if it leaves us both anxious and confused, perhaps it is our sense of ethics that needs to be deepened and enlarged. Perhaps we need a richer, more exciting, more compelling, and eminently more personal understanding of the moral life. Friendship offers this. It helps us see that ethics is not a solution we seek to a problem we wish we could avoid, but is our life lived in a certain way. Perhaps the best description of morality that fits the model of friendship is the one given by Etienne Gilson over fifty years ago: "Morals is the science of how man is to conduct himself so that the story of his life may have a happy ending," and this means, he concluded, that "care to shape his life towards a prosperous end is one with care to bring his own humanity to the very peak of achievement."[24]

Gilson's comments help us see that morality is not something apart from us—it is not a thing at all—but is rather the particular story we take our life to be because of the kind of person we want to become. It is the story of our happiness, but of a happiness achieved with others through a conformity to the good. It is a matter, Paul L. Holmer says, of coming to see "how we establish ourselves as persons. How do we get a peace that passes all understanding? How do we get rest for our souls?"[25] The moral life is trying to determine what kind of love brings us to fullness, what kind of devotion will make us whole. It is a study of how we become the very thing on which we have set our hearts. All this suggests that morality is not just part of life, it is the whole of life viewed a certain way, seen as the story of how men and women through their beliefs, convictions, and actions, through their loves, passions, and attachments, *together* make themselves into someone they had not been before. The moral life is the saga of the making and remaking of persons through a shared love. In this way, each of us is unmistakably moral because each of us is a person of desires, cares, and concerns, of goods we love and want to embody, of people with whom we hope to be one. The question then is not whether we are or can be moral, but whether what we desire can make us good.

All this may sound strangely remote from the rolling hills of eastern Missouri where this book began, but actually it has returned us to the thought with which the chapter commenced. Warrenton was a way of life designed to make a single possibility real; morality should do the same. Warrenton was an argument about the moral life; it witnessed that morality was making good on the purpose in which happiness and wholeness consists. It was a matter of desires, of passions and attachments, of an overwhelming, boundless, all-consuming love, but of all these channeled into a devotion by which we are transformed. The Christian moral life ought to do the same. Christian morality does not and ought not try to extirpate the passions, but should teach us to be passionate about God. It should not try to squelch our desires, but teach us to desire God more than we desire anything else. Christian morality is about a boundless, all-consuming love—it is about loving God passionately, with a hunger and thirst satisfied only by the intimacy we call friendship with God in the Kingdom of God. For a Christian, morality plots the transfiguration of the self unto holiness. It is a question of becoming godly, of being ruled by the Spirit, of being transformed by virtues born from charity's love. If the purpose of the Christian moral life is to make us like God so we can be happy with God, then morality is a matter not of problems but of the special love of charity that brings likeness to the God who is our peace.

But how do we gain the good that is our life? How do we grow in the love we are to master? Through friendships. We said before that we have access to the goods in which we are completed through friendships with those who share that desire. We do not reach our wholeness directly, it is mediated in relationships bounded by a good both seek. Fullness of life is something we receive in friendship with others. We can see this in good marriages, we can see it in those friendships without which we cannot imagine ourself, and, to a certain extent, we can even see it in those more casual friendships which may not be so enduring but which, nonetheless, shape us for life. Friendship is a fitting model for the moral life because it respects that the change of self necessary for wholeness is impossible apart from those relationships in which love for that wholeness can be shared. What made Warrenton memorable is the happiness and goodness it brought us, but both were the work of friendships, and those friendships were born from surrender to an adventure whose fullness was something we could individually desire but only mutually seek.

The moral life is the same. It is hunger and thirst for fullness, an unquenchable desire for peace, an endless longing for a healing. It is lifetime seeking for love. It is all this, but it is also friendship, because the fullness we seek can only be reached through others who seek it too. That is the moral life, a pilgrimage towards wholeness, a quest on which we notice many others are searching as well. It is our common search that brings us together as friends, but

it is our friendship that brings us what we seek. The diffi-
culty with so many contemporary approaches to the moral
life is that it is exactly this crucial dimension of the moral
life they overlook. The rest of the book will explore how
our understanding of the moral life takes shape when friendship is its center. Aristotle was among the first to consider
this, so it is his vision of the moral life, particularly his
understanding of a good and flourishing life, we shall consider next.

2. A Look at Aristotle's Ethics:

A Search for the Center That Did Not Hold

I. A Little Prelude: A World in Disarray

At the beginning of Walker Percy's novel *Love in the Ruins,* Dr. Thomas More muses on a crazy, broken-down world, a world in which "the center did not hold."[1] More has invented the lapsometer which he hopes will help put the world back together: "With it, my little invention, in hand, any doctor can probe the very secrets of the soul, diagnose the maladies that poison the wellsprings of man's hope."[2]

But the maladies run deep. In that world of Paradise Estates, Love Clinics, Geriatric Rehabilitation Centers, and Euphoria Switches, people whose lives have been expertly programmed for happiness die with the same longings with which they were born. Dr. More tells the story of a lady who was "in truth terrified by her well-nigh perfect life, really death in life, in Paradise, where all her needs were satisfied and all she had to do was play golf and bridge and sit around the clubhouse watching swim-meets and the Christian baton-twirlers." This woman who "woke every morning to a perfect husband, perfect children, a perfect life," still "shook like a leaf with morning terror."[3]

Despite the advantages of inhabiting the best of all worlds, the citizens of Paradise Estates die with a chilling kind of emptiness. They die without ever having bridged "the dread chasm that has rent the soul of Western man

27

ever since the famous philosopher Descartes ripped body loose from mind and turned the very soul into a ghost that haunts its own house."[4] Dr. Thomas More sees the problem, but he is hardly better off; indeed, the reason he is able to help so many people is that he, too, leads "a fairly miserable life."[5] Like so many others in Paradise Estates, he is plagued with nostalgia for a life he does not know how to retrieve and boredom with a life whose perfection he does not really believe.

Several times in the novel More reflects that he was content in those days when he "went to mass with Samantha, happy as a man could be, ate Christ and held him to his word, if you eat me you'll have life in you, so I had life in me."[6] But he had quit going to Mass and so had most everyone else. Of the priest Father Smith, More says, "There is little to be said about Father Smith since he is in no way remarkable, having been a good and faithful if undistinguished priest for twenty-five years, having baptized the newborn into a new life, married lovers, shriven sinners, comforted the sick, visited the poor and imprisoned, anointed the dying, buried the dead."[7]

And yet, these duties are all pretty remarkable when we remember they represent a way of life clustered around a Word which gave it purpose. All those things Father Rinaldo Smith did seem inconsequential until it is noticed they are rooted in a conviction about life and what must happen to us if that life is not to be lost. The citizens of Paradise Estates have pretty much forgotten Father Smith and his ragtag lot of parishioners. Nobody bothers them, few take them seriously, most have not the faintest idea what they are doing every Sunday morning when they gather in the restored slave quarters which serves as their church. But they are the most important people in the novel because what they do every Sunday and throughout the rest of their lives makes them the people through whom a love that is in ruins can be restored.

Interestingly, this image of a world in ruins is also one

with which Alasdair MacIntyre begins his pivotal work, *After Virtue*. MacIntyre opens the book with the "disquieting suggestion" that our moral world has not changed, it is gone. Like *Love in the Ruins*, he speaks of a world in which something has been lost, a world without gist or center. He offers the analogy of a disaster in the natural sciences. "Widespread riots occur, laboratories are burnt down, physicists are lynched, books and instruments are destroyed. Finally a Know-Nothing political movement takes power and successfully abolishes science teaching in schools and universities, imprisoning and executing the remaining scientists."[8] After a time "enlightened people" realize the mistake and "seek to revive science," but that is nearly impossible, too much has been lost. "All they possess," MacIntyre writes, "are fragments: a knowledge of experiments detached from any knowledge of the theoretical context which gave them significance; parts of theories unrelated either to the other bits and pieces of theory which they possess or to experiment; instruments whose use has been forgotten; half-chapters from books, single pages from articles, not always fully legible because torn and charred." Despite the desire to put the natural sciences back together again, "those contexts which would be needed to make sense of what they are doing have been lost, perhaps irretrievably."[9]

The same catastrophe, MacIntyre suggests, has happened to morality. "But of course in saying this," MacIntyre explains, "I am not merely contending that morality is not what it once was, but also and more importantly that what once was morality has to some large degree disappeared—and that this marks a degeneration, a grave cultural loss."[10] We continue to use moral language, make judgments, and come to decisions, but it is difficult for us to explain why we decide one thing over another because the context in which our decisions would be intelligible is precisely what is missing. "Up to the present in everyday discourse," MacIntyre comments, "the habit of speaking of moral judgments as true or false persists; but the question of what it is in virtue of which a particular moral judgment is true or false has come to lack any clear answer."[11] Like our counterparts in the scientific disaster, we have bits and pieces, but what we lack is a center which would allow us to make sense of the whole. Consequently, our efforts to proceed morally are marked by frustration rooted in an inescapable arbitrariness. It is because of this, MacIntyre explains, that "we have—very largely—lost our comprehension, both theoretical and practical, of morality."[12]

We have inherited a morality that is best described as "after virtue" inasmuch as the classical moral traditions of Aristotle and Aquinas were jettisoned by the Enlightenment project to establish a rational foundation for an objective morality for which the theistic backdrop had disappeared. MacIntyre, however, is "after virtue" precisely because the Enlightenment project has failed.[13] The argument of the book is that an ethic of virtue must be retrieved if morality is to be restored. If there is a way to move beyond this barren terrain, it is by turning back to an ethic of virtue, specifically the ethics of Aristotle. *After Virtue* takes us forward by turning us back. In no way does MacIntyre suggest we can uncritically endorse everything Aristotle held; for instance, there is an elitism in his ethic a Christian account of the moral life certainly must challenge. But MacIntyre does hold something like Aristotle's ethic of virtue must be recovered if our fragmented moral world is to be made whole. As he explains, "But all these historical truths, crucial as they are, are unimportant compared with the fact that Aristotelianism is philosophically the most powerful of pre-modern modes of moral thought. If a pre-modern view of morals and politics is to be vindicated against modernity, it will be in something like Aristotelian terms or not at all."[14]

In our terms, it is within the embrace of an Aristotelian virtue approach to the moral life that the role of friendship is best understood. Like MacIntyre, the argument of this book is that if we are to move beyond "love in the ruins," a world in which everyone is nice but few are happy, we must restore a center that has been lost. One way to begin this retrieval is to return to an account of the moral life clustered around a specific understanding of the purpose of human nature and the virtues necessary to achieve it. That is how Aristotle thought about morality, and it is in that context that the necessity and purpose of friendship will be most clearly seen.

II. Making Good on Life's Purpose: What Aristotle's Ethic Is All About

One of the more interesting, if sobering, moral exercises is to consider the many ways a human life can go wrong. A chilling meditation to be sure, for it reminds us how easy it is to adopt patterns of behavior which seem so incidental in themselves, yet stretched over the years can leave us a lifetime away from where we ought to be. However, it was exactly an awareness of this possibility that structured Aristotle's understanding of ethics. Aristotle believed a human life could be wasted. Put negatively, the most basic moral question is this: "How must we live if we are not to end up with a life we ultimately regret?" Put positively, the most basic moral question is: "What is the best way of life and how should we live if we are going to achieve it?"[15] That morality be born from the question, "How ought we to live?" indicates that the scope of Aristotle's ethic was far wider than an occasional decision to make or problem to solve; indeed, morality was the arena where persons were made or broken, where lives succeeded or were lost, and the worst fate for any human being was an early death. To die young was not to have lived long enough to make good on life's purpose, and for Aristotle that was tragic.

It is commonly noted that Aristotle's ethic is teleological, a Greek word meaning end, goal, or completion. The 'telos' of a life represents that life's fullness, the good which has to be embodied for a life to become what it needs to become if it is not to fall short of the very thing for which life is given. This is strange language to our ears, but only because we are not accustomed to normative understandings of life. A teleological ethic such as Aristotle's argues that life is given to achieve something, a matter of making good on some purpose it is the meaning of life to complete. The teleological language of goal, purpose, and aim underscores the conviction that to be human is to have some good to become, some good into which we must grow and according to which we must be formed if we are to understand what being human means at all. In a teleological approach to ethics, being human is not something we are naturally, but something we become by embodying the good in which human fullness resides. It is not just the case that ethics concerns the making of persons, but more precisely that there is something specific, something highly exact, that must happen to a person if his or her life is not to be judged a failure.

The telos is intrinsic to human nature, a purpose stitched into the fabric of life. It is not a matter of choice, but the very thing for which life is given. For Aristotle then, to be human is to have a purpose on which to make good, and not to do that, to ignore or deny it, is not just to become something different, but to fail at the very thing for which life is given; truly, to fail on the telos is never to have existed at all. In a teleological ethic the central moral question is always the same: What must I do with myself if my life is not to be judged a failure? To have a morality is to have an answer to that question.

The implication is clear. In order to be there is something we have to become. It is not enough to be, simply to exist, for existence requires the transformation of the self into the good by which existence is defined. To exist is to become something more, it is life qualified by the purpose and goal which represent its completeness. In a teleological ethic, being implies becoming, and becoming implies the appropriation of a good which enables moral existence. As MacIntyre explains, for Aristotle the moral life was not primarily a question of options; nor, like modern liberalism, were questions "about the good life . . . or the ends of human life" seen to be "systematically unsettleable," choices that could be preferred but not rationally justified.[16] No, for Aristotle "questions about the good life" or the "ends of human life" ultimately had to be settleable for it is only when these were identified that we could form the kinds of attachments by which we are brought into being. In short, to be was to be for something, and the telos represented precisely what that something was, namely the good the possession of which was human fullness. Human nature was not given, it was achieved; it was a wholeness to accomplish by the kind of life and activities, which Aristotle called the virtues, by which human beings were constituted. As MacIntyre explains,

> Within that teleological scheme there is a fundamental contrast between man-as-he-happens-to-be and man-as-he-could-be-if-he-realises-his-essential-nature. Ethics is the science which is to enable men to understand how they make the transition from the former state to the latter. . . . The precepts which enjoin the various virtues and prohibit the vices which are their counterparts instruct us how to move from potentiality to act, how to realise our true nature and to reach our true end. To defy them will be to be frustrated and incomplete, to fail to achieve that good of rational happiness which it is peculiarly ours as a species to pursue. . . . We thus have a threefold scheme in which human-nature-as-it-happens-to-be (human nature in its untutored state) is initially discrepant and discordant with the precepts of ethics and needs to be transformed by the instruction of practical reason and experience into human-nature-as-it-could-be-if-it-realised-its-telos.[17]

The telos obviously represents human fullness and flourishing, but what exactly is it? Aristotle is trying to identify the highest good of human life, an unsurpassable good the possession of which represents complete well-being. As he understands it, to have this good is to be lacking in nothing, for the telos is not only the goal or project of a life, it is also its end point, a perfection which cannot be exceeded; therefore, to possess this good is to desire no more. Aristotle calls this unsurpassable good "eudaimonia," and although it is commonly translated "happiness," that is misleading. As J. L. Ackrill notes, "The word eudaimonia has a force not at all like 'happiness,' 'comfort,' or 'pleasure,' but more like 'the best possible life' (where 'best' has not a narrowly moral sense). This is why there can be plenty of disagreement as to what form of life is eudaimonia, but no disagreement that eudaimonia is what we all want."[18]

That is exactly Aristotle's point. Since eudaimonia is the fulsome good beyond which nothing more can be desired, it is the only thing desired for its own sake and not for the sake of something else.[19] Aristotle's identification of the telos as eudaimonia is based on an observation about human nature. Aristotle notes that we are active beings, we do many things every day: we work, we study, we recreate, we spend time with ourselves and others. Every human life is a tapestry of diverse, changing activities. And yet if we looked closely at all these activities we would find threaded through them a common desire which expresses the fundamental intention of our lives: we hunger for a completion, a wholeness to which each of these activities contributes a part, but is not the wholeness itself. Each of them is performed for a specific reason which identifies the action and its purpose, as well as its own special goodness. We eat and sleep in order to safeguard our health. We work in order to support ourselves and because often our work brings meaning into our lives. We study because we wish to learn, we recreate because we seek diversion. Each of these activities has its own special purpose, but they also share a common purpose, they are essential elements in what we take to be a good life. None of them alone comprises a good life, but all of them together contribute to a fullness we think will bring peace to our desires. Eudaimonia is the good "for the sake of which everything else is done."[20]

We catch Aristotle's logic. He is searching for the final good, that beyond which there is no further good to be gained. What characterizes each of the activities detailed above is that they are good, but in themselves they are not good enough to quiet the heart's desire for fullness. Although they are necessary to a complete life, no life would be complete that had them but nothing more. The reason, as Aristotle sees it, is that all these activities are done not only because of the distinctive goodness they mediate, whether that be learning, rest, prosperity, or companionship, but also for that greater good to which they contribute. They are necessary for wholeness, but are not themselves wholeness; even though they contain their own special good, they are not themselves the final good, but are a means towards it. That is why, as the people of Paradise Estates showed us, to have a life of all these goods is still to be haunted by a hunger for something more. For Aristotle this good is the final good, and it represents not only the one thing sought for its own sake and not for the sake of something else, but also that fullness for which everything else, however good, is done.

> The highest good, on the other hand, must be something final. Thus, if there is only one final end, this will be the good we are seeking; if there are several, it will be the most final and perfect of them. We call that which is pursued as an end in itself more final than an end which is pursued for the sake of something else; and what is never chosen as a means to something else we call more final than that which is chosen both as an end in itself and as a means to something else. What is always chosen as an end in itself and never as a means to something else is called final in an unqualified sense. This description seems to apply to happiness [eudaimonia] above all else: for we always choose happiness [eudaimonia] as an end

in itself and never for the sake of something else. Honor, pleasure, intelligence, and all virtue we choose partly for themselves—for we would choose each of them even if no further advantage would accrue from them—but we also choose them partly for the sake of happiness [eudaimonia], because we assume that it is through them that we will be happy. On the other hand, no one chooses happiness [eudaimonia] for the sake of honor, pleasure, and the like, nor as a means to anything at all.[21]

As J. L. Ackrill writes, Aristotle makes two points about eudaimonia: "(i) you cannot say of eudaimonia that you seek it for the sake of anything else, you can say of anything else that you seek it for the sake of eudaimonia; (ii) you cannot say you would prefer eudaimonia plus something extra to eudaimonia."[22] These two points are connected. "For if you could say that you would prefer eudaimonia plus something extra to eudaimonia, you could say that you sought eudaimonia for the sake of something else, namely the greater end consisting of eudaimonia plus something extra."[23] If eudaimonia was sought for the sake of something else and not for its own sake, it would not be eudaimonia—we would be confused about the final good—because that very 'moreness' being added to eudaimonia would indicate there was still some greater, more comprehensive good beyond what we had attained. There would be an incompleteness to our understanding of eudaimonia, something about that composite of goods that could not properly be called final precisely because it left us dissatisfied. If eudaimonia refers to the best possible life, and in that sense is the 'final good,' there can be no good that falls outside it. If there is, we have yet to identify eudaimonia properly.

Still, this greater, more comprehensive good need not be a single good. Ackrill stresses that when Aristotle speaks of eudaimonia as the final good, this need not imply there is some "'single object of desire' in the sense of a monolithic as opposed to 'inclusive' end,"[24] but suggests rather that "eudaimonia is the most desirable sort of life, the life that contains all intrinsically worthwhile activities."[25] Eudaimonia is not a single good, but includes "all intrinsic goods."[26] Aristotle admits this when he speaks of eudaimonia as "the most final and perfect" of all final ends.[27] What Aristotle implies is that there are several 'final' goods inasmuch as there are many intrinsically good activities without which no life can be complete, but eudaimonia is properly the 'most final' of all because it is exactly all these goods taken together in a single way of life. It is the 'most final' of the 'final' goods inasmuch as none of them alone can be counted the highest good, but no life can be good without them.

Thus, eudaimonia is not a single highest good, some particular good which surpasses all others, but the kind of life in which all those intrinsic goods are included. These, taken together, comprise eudaimonia for they enable human flourishing, they constitute the best possible life, and that is what eudaimonia is, "the complete and perfectly satisfying life."[28] As Ackrill explains, "'most final' meant 'final without qualification' and referred to the comprehensive end that includes all partial ends."[29] It referred to all those goods which make "life desirable and lacking in nothing." Eudaimonia does just that. For, Aristotle says, we regard it as "the most worthwhile of all things, not being counted as one good thing among others."[30] In short, "eudaimonia, being absolutely final and genuinely self-sufficient, is more desirable than anything else in that it includes everything desirable in itself. It is best, and better than anything else," Ackrill explains, "not in the way that bacon is better than eggs and than tomatoes (and therefore the best of the three to choose), but in the way that bacon, eggs, and tomatoes is a better breakfast than either bacon or eggs or tomatoes— and is indeed the best breakfast without qualification."[31]

To speak of eudaimonia as the "best life without qualification" implies there is some substantive meaning to what the best life is. That is exactly how Aristotle understood it.

When he speaks of eudaimonia as "that which taken by itself makes life something desirable and deficient in nothing,"[32] he does not mean that what counts as eudaimonia is whatever any person finds desirable. Indeed, one of the most pressing signs of moral weakness for Aristotle is never learning to desire the right things, never learning to take pleasure in what is good. Aristotle knows there is much disagreement over what eudaimonia is, but he traces that confusion not to the complexity of eudaimonia, but to a general lack of virtue. For him, eudaimonia has a definite, normative meaning. It represents not just a way of life which is lacking in nothing because it satisfies one's desires, for indeed they may be improper desires, but, more exactly, a life that can satisfy the desires of the good person precisely because it is capable of making her good. Eudaimonia is not an empty, formless concept each person is free to identify through whatever desires he or she wants fulfilled. On the contrary, eudaimonia is the most desirable of lives because it satisfies the person who desires nothing more than to become good.

That is why Ackrill is right that *happiness*, though a common translation, "is not a proper translation" of eudaimonia.[33] To speak of eudaimonia simply as happiness is misleading because it suggests eudaimonia is whatever makes one happy, irrespective of what that happiness is. But Aristotle will not accept that. He admitted that many people in his city-state of Athens make of eudaimonia what they want, commonly defining it according to whatever gives them pleasure, but that is not an argument against his account of eudaimonia as much as it is testimony to their lack of moral development. He admits that "the common run of people and the most vulgar identify it [eudaimonia] with pleasure, and for that reason are satisfied with a life of enjoyment,"[34] but that only indicates they have never understood what happiness and well-being involve. It is not pleasure alone that makes one happy, but taking pleasure in the best possible things.

In this way, Aristotle does not contrast pleasure and goodness, but neither does he allow pleasure to be independent of goodness. He admits pleasure is something for which everyone aims, but genuine pleasure can be neither recognized nor experienced apart from virtue; indeed, it is the truly good person who has the greatest pleasures. As Julia Annas explains in her essay, "Aristotle on Pleasure and Goodness," "Now Aristotle does say that pleasure is the natural end of all animate beings (1172b5–1173a5), and he thinks it absurd to deny that pleasure is a good, because, he holds, everyone does, in fact, aim at pleasure (1153b25–31). But he cannot be a hedonist, because he cannot hold that pleasure is one single independently specifiable end which everyone pursues regardless of how they set about it."[35]

Aristotle cannot be a hedonist because he does not declare every pleasure good, and even though he does agree that in the life of every person pleasure is sought, he does not conclude that pleasure, therefore, is the purpose of life. For Aristotle the virtues comprise the telos of human life for they are the qualities of goodness which bring every person to fullness. The fact that the virtues are the good life regardless of whether one finds pleasure in them indicates that for Aristotle genuine pleasure is not a matter of immediate satisfaction, nor certainly of personal whim, but is something one can experience precisely to the degree he or she becomes virtuous. Like the virtues, genuine pleasure has to be learned, it is something that must be attained, and it can never be separated from goodness. For Aristotle, pleasure accompanies the virtuous life, it describes the person who truly delights in the good; thus, it is secondary to and derivative of the virtues because it is only when one becomes good that he or she knows what genuine pleasure is. As Annas explains, "For Aristotle, one cannot pursue pleasure regardless of the moral worth of the actions that are one's means to getting it. Rather it is the other way round: it is one's conception of the good life which determines what

counts for one as being pleasant."[36] Aristotle does not reject
pleasure, he simply insists that in order to recognize what
is genuinely pleasant one must be genuinely good. People
may find pleasure outside the virtuous life, but they are as
mistaken about pleasure as they are about the meaning of
life. Pleasure is real only where the good has been culti-
vated; it is their lack of virtue that makes their pleasure
counterfeit.

> Only the truly good man will perform the actions required by
> virtue without objection or strain and feel the right kind of
> pleasure in doing them. . . . So the good life and the truly
> pleasant life must be explained in terms of one another. . . .
> Goodness does not consist in avoiding pleasure in the interests
> of some higher ideal but in being right about what is truly
> pleasant. What is required is not asceticism but intelligent
> choice that brings with it the redirection of pleasure to what
> is chosen. Learning to be virtuous involves learning to take
> pleasure in virtuous activities; the latter is not something
> added on to the former but is part of it and bound up with it.[37]

Aristotle cannot separate eudaimonia from the virtues.
For him eudaimonia does not represent the satisfaction of
individual desires, the fulfillment of personal wants and
preferences, nor the achievement of self-interest, unless
those desires, wants, preferences, and interests are for genuine goodness. Eudaimonia is the virtuous life. The good
person knows, Aristotle reasons, that "since happiness is
one of the most divine things,"[38] it must be "some kind
of activity of the soul in conformity with virtue."[39] That is
why eudaimonia is not the reward of the virtuous life, but
how the virtuous life is best described. Eudaimonia and the
virtues are intrinsically connected. It is not the prize of the
virtues; rather, eudaimonia is the virtuous life in its fullest
and most complete form. As Ackrill puts it, "It [eudaimo-
nia] is doing well, not the result of doing well; a life, not
the reward of a life."[40] It "'must be the activity of a complete life in accordance with complete virtue.' The reference

to whole and part makes clear that by 'complete virtue' here is meant all virtues."[41] Leaving aside the question of whether any single life can display all the virtues,[42] it is clear that for Aristotle the telos of human life is intrinsically connected to the activity of the virtues. MacIntyre puts this well:

> The virtues are precisely those qualities the possession of which will enable an individual to achieve eudaimonia and the lack of which will frustrate his movement toward that telos. But although it would not be incorrect to describe the exercise of virtues as a means to the end of achieving the good for man, that description is ambiguous. . . . For what constitutes the good for man is a complete human life lived at its best, and the exercise of the virtues is a necessary and central part of such a life, not a mere preparatory exercise to secure such a life. We thus cannot characterise the good for man adequately without already having made reference to the virtues. And within an Aristotelian framework the suggestion therefore that there might be some means to achieve the good for man without the exercise of the virtues makes no sense.[43]

MacIntyre's comments are helpful for two reasons. First, they remind us that for Aristotle the business of morality is the making and remaking of persons. To develop the virtues is to see it is not enough just to be human, for to know what it means to be human one must also become good. To be human is to be virtuous, that is the thrust of the *Nichomachean Ethics*. An ethics of virtue always suggests something crucial to human wholeness is lacking, that something more has to be done if a person is ever to be established. To be human is to make good on the purpose or telos of our life, it is to achieve that for which our nature is given.

Aristotle touches this when he says to be human is to have some special function to achieve. Just as the function of a flute player, he observes, is to play the flute well, "so the goodness and performance of man would seem to reside in whatever is his proper function."[44] As Thomas Nagel comments about this passage, when Aristotle speaks of the function or 'ergon' of a human being, he is identifying exactly that special thing human beings do that makes us who we are. "The 'ergon' of a thing, in general," Nagel writes, "is what it does that makes it what it is. . . . When something has an 'ergon', that thing's good is specified by it. The proper 'ergon' of man, by which human excellence is measured, is that which makes him a man rather than anything else."[45] The implication, of course, is that not to achieve this function is not to be. For Aristotle, human and moral development are the same, and they occur only through the ongoing exercise of this 'ergon.'

The proper function of men and women is the best thing they can do, specifically whatever activity or set of activities sets them apart from other creatures and brings them to themselves. For Aristotle, we know, this is the virtuous life. The virtuous life is the best thing we can do because it is precisely in doing the virtues that we are brought to our best and most promising self. As Aristotle summarizes,

> On these assumptions, if we take the proper function of man to be a certain kind of life, and if this kind of life is an activity of the soul and consists in actions performed in conjunction with the rational element, and if a man of high standards is he who performs these actions well and properly, and if a function is well performed when it is performed in accordance with the excellence appropriate to it; we reach the conclusion that the good of man is an activity of the soul in conformity with excellence or virtue, and if there are several virtues, in conformity with the best and most complete.[46]

Secondly, MacIntyre's analysis of the relationship between the virtues and eudaimonia also suggests the telos is not so much something towards which we move, but something in which we participate. True, the telos represents the goal, the fulsome meaning of life. While it can also be said that we advance toward that end through the virtues, the movement implied is not a change of place but a change of person. For Aristotle, a person moves toward the telos by being changed according to it. Eudaimonia represents not something far off, but exactly how persons are transformed by their best and noblest activities. This is a movement of interior transformation, and that is why we can speak of the virtues as a kind of conversion; they are the ongoing formation of our life according to its fullness. The more perfectly and completely this transformation occurs in us the happier we are, since in such assimilation to the good there is less discrepancy between who we are and who we need to become. This is why for Aristotle our telos, eudaimonia, and the virtues are finally one. Our telos is eudaimonia, and eudaimonia is the virtuous life. As MacIntyre puts it, "Aristotle takes the telos of human life to be a certain kind of life; the telos is not something to be achieved at some future point, but in the way our whole life is construed."[47]

Does the achievement of the telos require the company of friends? It is odd that in such a lengthy examination of Aristotle's ethics we have yet to mention friendship, but up to this point Aristotle has been silent on it too. In the first seven books of the *Nichomachean Ethics* Aristotle offers a detailed account of eudaimonia and goodness, he presents his treatise on the virtues, he explores the mystery of human weakness or 'akrasia,' he examines the meaning of justice, and he describes the qualities of his paragon of virtue, the Athenian gentleman or the 'high-minded man.' In all this there is hardly a mention of friendship. Aristotle does talk about the qualities of friendliness in Book IV, but in no way does he indicate friendship is integral to his understanding of the moral life. In fact, one could close the *Nichomachean Ethics* at the end of Book VII with the reasonable conclusion that the constitutive elements of Aristotle's ethics are already firmly in place.

But he would be mistaken. A curious turn occurs in Book VIII. Aristotle begins to talk of friendship, and what is strange is not only that he waits so long to introduce it, but that he speaks as if everything he has so far written has prepared the reader for this topic. He begins to speak of friendship as if it were exactly what we were expecting. At the outset of Book VIII he writes, "Continuing in a sequence, the next subject which we shall have to discuss is friendship."[48] We are interested, but we are also perplexed. Where is the sequence? How has anything Aristotle thus far said entailed this transition to friendship? Clearly something has happened between Book VII and Book VIII of the *Ethics,* but Aristotle has not told us what it is. Perhaps a clue is in remembering just what kind of book the *Nichomachean Ethics* is.

Strictly speaking, the *Nichomachean Ethics* is not a book on the moral life, but a series of lecture notes which Aristotle wrote, developed, and revised over many years of teaching. It does not represent the culmination of those years, but is, rather, an ongoing account of what Aristotle was thinking, of how his own thought changed and shifted not only through the experience of teaching, but also through the impact of his changing world. The *Nichomachean Ethics* represents not a polished summary of Aristotle's academic career, but the twists and turns of a man's thought challenged, stretched and redefined through all those messy experiences of life which refuse to fit the categories we assign them. That the *Nichomachean Ethics* details the development and maturation of Aristotle's thought through the crucible of teaching explains the occasional lapses and repetitions that mark the *Ethics,* but it also explains what makes reading this work so fascinating. The *Nichomachean Ethics* is thick with life, no stodgy masterpiece; its appeal is precisely how much the gritty world of Athens keeps breaking in.

What we see in the *Nichomachean Ethics* is not a man who writes at a safe distance from a world he is trying to explain, but a man who both wrestles with and is frustrated by a world whose impact he neither can nor wishes to avoid. The *Nichomachean Ethics* impresses because of what it does not deny. Aristotle does not flinch from the impact of Athens on his ethics. The real world does break in, and that Aristotle responds accordingly may well explain why his discussion of the moral life has such force for us today.

It is exactly the dialogue between Aristotle's thought and the human drama raging in Athens that accounts for the curious turn to friendship in Book VIII. There Aristotle suggests a connection between the activity of friendship and the acquisition and growth of the virtues he has not hinted at before. In this chapter we have explored Aristotle's understanding of the purpose of human life, the virtues, and the goods in which life finds completion, but we have not suggested all this depends on special kinds of friendships that make the good life possible. In Book VIII of his *Ethics* this is precisely the argument Aristotle advances. We cannot have the virtues apart from the kinds of friendships which make acquiring them and flourishing in them possible. Why Aristotle's argument takes this turn, and what he means by friendship—its status and role in the moral life—is what we shall consider next.

3. Aristotle on Friendship:

What It Means for the Moral Life

I. From the 'Polis' to Friendship: Why Aristotle Makes That Move

The *Nichomachean Ethics* ends far from where it began. It ends in a discussion of friendship, but it began in posing a relationship between morality and politics. The moral life is a function of the polis, for it represents not the individual's, but the community's pursuit of the good, the community's commitment to discover, embody, and sustain the virtues.[1] The goal of the moral life is not just the virtuous person, but the virtuous community.

Morality is connected to the polis for a second reason. It is not only the case that the aim of ethics is the virtuous city-state, but that each person needs the support and companionship of society if her or his growth in the good is to be possible. Implicitly, we see the seeds of Aristotle's eventual argument for friendship. The connection he forges between ethics and politics suggests that each person's good can be attained only in the society or fellowship one has with others who seek the same good. The moral life aims to achieve a certain kind of society, namely a society of virtue, but it also requires a certain kind of society, the society of men and women dedicated to the same telos, working for and with one another to make each person's achievement of that good possible. In this sense, the polis or city-state is both the prerequisite of the moral life and its ultimate aim. It is a prerequisite inasmuch as a society of people dedicated to virtue is required to make the virtuous life possible, and it is the aim of the moral life inasmuch as the virtuous city-state, the commonwealth of virtue, is, for Aristotle, the most perfect representation of human flourishing.

Ideally, the city-state ought to be a community of friends, the locus of civic friendship. As Alasdair MacIntyre explains this civic friendship, "We are to think then of friendship as being the sharing of all in the common project of creating and sustaining the life of the city, a sharing incorporated in the immediacy of an individual's particular friendships."[2] The city-state should cluster around a bond between citizens, a bond which both presupposes and reflects "a wide range of agreement in that community" on the good life and the virtues required to achieve it.[3] "The type of friendship which Aristotle has in mind," MacIntyre explains, "is that which embodies a shared recognition of and pursuit of a good. It is this sharing which is essential and primary to the constitution of any form of community, whether that of a household or that of a city."[4]

That Aristotle understood ethics to be in the service of the city-state, and the city-state to be civic friendship, helps us understand why, later in the *Nichomachean Ethics,* when he begins to discuss friendship explicitly, he is lifting up something which was present in his account of the moral life all along. Prior to Book VIII, Aristotle does not treat friendship directly, but he does presume it as descriptive of the city-state. In Book VIII, however, Aristotle brings friendship to the fore, and argues for it as an ingredient to the moral life, precisely because he doubts, in the polis, this commitment to the common good and the virtuous life. In acknowledging the loss of civic friendship rooted in the weakening of a consensus about the nature of the good life and the virtues it requires, Aristotle does not reject friendship as the locus for the virtuous life, he finds it a new home. Near the end of the *Nichomachean Ethics,* he speaks

not of the friendship of the polis, but of the friendships of
people committed to virtue. A shift occurs—not a shift
from the polis to friendship, but from one kind of friendship to another, from civic friendship to the smaller community of friends who want to be good.

Aristotle argues in the first part of the *Ethics* that growth
in the virtues requires a community committed to virtue.
However, if such a polity ceases to exist, then not only does
the policy change, but so, too, does the individual's possibility for virtue. Aristotle knows there can be no person of
virtue without others in relationship to whom such a life
can be pursued.

Initially, Aristotle wants Athens to function as the community in which the virtues can be acquired and he begins
his *Ethics* by placing morality at the service of the city-state.
However, as those lectures unfold, there is a crescendo of
frustration. He does not want to contrast the polis with
friendship because for him the polis ought to be friendship;
however, that such is not the case in Athens becomes increasingly clear.[5] Near the end of the *Ethics* Aristotle admits
Athens is not the virtuous city-state he would like it to be,
indeed, it is not clear it ever was; rather, "each man lives
as he pleases, 'dealing out law to his children and his wife'
as the Cyclopes do."[6] It is only in Sparta that Aristotle sees
a polity strong enough to sustain the virtuous life, and that
only frustrates him the more because he feels Sparta has the
wrong virtues.[7]

Aristotle has come to see that in Athens the commitment
to the common good of a just society is absent, and without
it the moral life is impossible. With "each man living as
he pleases," Athens is in the same fragmented state as the
imaginary world with which Alasdair MacIntyre opens *After
Virtue*. The commitment to virtue for which Aristotle
hoped is a fiction, the city-state is not what he took it to
be, and this is alarming because it means he lacks the community necessary for the virtuous life to be real. "Now the
best thing would be," Aristotle acknowledges, "to make

the correct care of these matters a common concern. But if the community neglects them, it would seem to be incumbent upon every man to help his children and friends attain virtue."[8]

A significant change takes place with that remark. Precisely because the city-state no longer enables but actually frustrates the acquisition and nurturing of the virtues, Aristotle searches for another way to develop them, and his search takes him to friendship. By the end of the *Nichomachean Ethics*, friendship has replaced the polis as the context in which the virtues are learned and embodied. This move represents not so much a change in the structure of Aristotle's ethics, as much as a shift in its focus. The overall structure of Aristotle's ethics, and its constitutive elements of telos, eudaimonia, and the virtues, remains, but exactly what these mean, how they are related, and how they function, shift in light of this focus on friendship. That this is the case is suggested by Aristotle's otherwise enigmatic invitation at the end of the *Nichomachean Ethics*, "So let us begin our discussion."[9] Having reached the end, what are we to begin? Could it be that Aristotle asks us to reread his lectures from the perspective of friendship? Is this an invitation to return to the discussion of eudaimonia, the good life and the virtues, thinking now of friendship, not the polis, as the rubric under which each of these elements of the moral life is best understood?

This is not to suggest Aristotle abandons the polis. Quite the contrary, he needs the polis to keep friendship from stagnation. His is not an ethics of retreat or withdrawal. The relationship between friendship and the city-state, is not friendship removed from the polis, not even friendship over against the polis, but friendship within the polis.

As the locus for moral development, friendship may represent a critique of the city-state, but it also represents its hope, for it is only inasmuch as truly good people abound that the city-state is possible. Thus, there is reciprocity between friendship and the city-state. Friendship is the soil for virtue, the relationship in which a goodness not possible within society-at-large can be attained. Friendship needs the city-state, not only as the larger setting in which virtues, particularly justice, can be exercised, but also because the questioning and challenge of the polis is necessary to stretch the virtues to greater levels of goodness. Without the community of friendship, the city-state would have no hope, but without the city-state, friendships would become too private, friends would be inclined to think their friendships exist for their own sake, and not for the city-state to which they are to summon justice.

If Aristotle's claim that we cannot have the virtues without a community dedicated to acquiring them is sound, then Athens's dilemma becomes our own. If our reflections in chapter one are at least minimally accurate, agreement on the good is difficult to spot in a culture whose morality is so individualistic and capricious. Put differently, is our society any more capable of enabling the virtuous life than Aristotle's Athens?

In a now famous passage at the end of *After Virtue,* Alasdair MacIntyre bemoans a society that has brought not virtue and enlightenment, but barbarism and darkness. In response, he calls for "the construction of new forms of community within which the moral life could be sustained so that both morality and civility might survive the coming ages of barbarism and darkness."[10] For MacIntyre, Aristotle's problem is our own. Society cannot endure without a community committed to the flourishing of goodness, but if such a community does not exist at-large, which seems to be the case in our very pluralistic society, then what must be found are those smaller societies whose commitment to virtue becomes a leaven for the well-being of the larger world. This is what makes friendship as a model for the moral life not only appealing, but crucial. Aristotle's concern is not quaint, for without the company of people who share a commitment to discovering and pursuing the good, it is impossible to escape the catastrophe MacIntyre sees already upon us. As he writes, "This time however the barbarians are not waiting beyond the frontiers; they have already been governing us for quite some time."[11] Aristotle's answer to the barbarians, to all those who "live as they please," was to turn to the friendships of good people who want to be better. That may point a way out of the darkness for us, so it is pressing that we understand exactly what Aristotle means.

II. Friendship: What It Means and Why We Need Them to Be Good

For Aristotle there are three kinds of friendship, each defined by what attracts persons and binds them together in friendship. There are friendships of pleasure, friendships of usefulness or advantage, and friendships based on goodness and virtue. Each friendship is constituted by the reason which brings the friends together in the first place, and is sustained by the ongoing pursuit of the good which joins them. As John M. Cooper remarks, "Aristotle counts the resulting relationships friendships of different types in virtue of the differences in what forms the bond between the associated parties."[12]

In the first two types of friendship, those based on pleasure and usefulness, Aristotle argues that people become friends not principally because they are attracted to one another, but because of the pleasure or usefulness they derive from the friendship. "Now, when the motive of the affection is usefulness," Aristotle writes, "the partners do not feel affection for one another per se but in terms of the good accruing to each from the other. The same is also true of those whose friendship is based on pleasure: we love witty people not for what they are, but for the pleasure they give us."[13] Aristotle agrees these are friendships, indeed very common ones, but only in a secondary sense, because the object of love is not the friend and her goodness, but the advantage a person gains in being a friend. These friendships usually end whenever that usefulness disappears. As Aristotle puts it,

> So we see that when the useful is the basis of affection, men love because of the good they get out of it, and when pleasure is the basis, for the pleasure they get out of it. In other words, the friend is loved not because he is a friend, but because he is useful or pleasant. Thus, these two kinds are friendships only incidentally, since the object of affection is not loved for being the kind of person he is, but for providing some good or pleasure. Consequently, such friendships are easily dissolved when the partners do not remain unchanged: the affection ceases as soon as one partner is no longer pleasant or useful to the other. Now, usefulness is not something permanent, but differs at different times. Accordingly, with the disappearance of the motive for being friends, the friendship, too, is dissolved, since the friendship owed its existence to these motives. [14]

Clearly, for Aristotle, "the central and basic kind of friendship" is what Cooper calls "friendship of character."[15] This is friendship constituted by the goodness and virtue of another. Each friendship is built up around the good the friends seek, and requires some similarity of interests, some agreement on likes and dislikes, and especially agreement on what one thinks is important. Friendships of character are the deepest and most permanent because they are constituted by an agreement on the good and a similarity in virtue. It is this shared love of the good that attracts the friends. In virtue friendships, each loves the other for his or her own sake because each loves the good, and the friend, to some degree, embodies that good; in short, they love one another because they are virtuous.

For Aristotle these friendships are marked by the deepest and most noble affection because their love is for the worthiest of objects, the "unqualified good" and how that shines in another.[16] Because there is this unity between what is loved and the person who is loved, between the good that is sought and the person who embodies it, character friendships best fulfill Aristotle's criteria for friendship: Each wishes the good of the friend for the sake of the friend.[17] Friendships are relationships of mutual well-wishing, each person being motivated from concern for the other's good. In character friendships this is best achieved because each shares the same good—to seek the other's good is to enhance one's own. Furthermore, since the more that good is sought the more it is embodied, the very good which binds the friends—this shared love for virtue—is what through love the friends become; hence, it is fitting that they love one another for his or her own sake, because each has more fully become the good in which both find joy. These are the best of friendships, the friendships of greatest moral importance, and Aristotle explains why:

> The perfect form of friendship is that between good men who are alike in excellence or virtue. For these friends wish alike for one another's good because they are good men, and they are good per se (that is, their goodness is something intrinsic, not incidental). Those who wish for their friends' good for their friends' sake are friends in the truest sense, since their attitude is determined by what their friends are and not by incidental considerations. Hence their friendship lasts as long as they are good, and that means it will last for a long time, since goodness or virtue is a thing that lasts. In addition, each partner is both good in the unqualified sense and good for his friend. For those who are good, i.e., good without qualification, are also beneficial to one another. . . . That such a friendship is lasting stands to reason, because in it are combined all the qualities requisite for people to be friends . . . and [it] has them per se, that is, as an essential part of the characters of the friends.[18]

Cooper makes two important observations about Aristotle's remark that "the perfect form of friendship is that between good men who are alike in excellence or virtue."

First, he spots a problem. Granted, for Aristotle, a friendship based on virtue is "perfect" because "it exhibits fully and perfectly all the characteristics that one reasonably expects a friendship to have,"[19] but does Aristotle imply "that only to fully virtuous persons—heroes of intellect and character—is it open to form a friendship of this basic kind"?[20] If so, Cooper continues, "it would follow, ordinary people, with the normal mixture of some good and some bad qualities of character, are not eligible partners for friendships of the basic type; they would be doomed, along with thoroughly bad people (1157a16—19, 1157b1–3; *EE* 1236b10–12, 1238a32–33), to having friendships of the other two types, at best. Does Aristotle mean to imply that one who is not completely virtuous can only be befriended for the sake of some pleasure or advantage he brings, that no one can associate with him (unless under deception: cf. 1165b8–15) for the sake of his good qualities of character?"[21] If this is the case, then the very relationships that are crucial for the moral life will be denied all except the already fully virtuous, and that puts Aristotle in an awkward position because he wants to argue that it is precisely in these friendships of virtue that the qualities constitutive of goodness are exercised and achieved. Friendships of moral goodness cannot be the preserve solely of those who have already achieved the good, but must also be the relationships in which people who want to be good can become good; in short, these are the relationships in which moral growth occurs. If Aristotle intends otherwise, if "perfect" friendship requires "perfect" people, then we are left with the depressing conclusion that eudaimonia, Aristotle's vision of the full and complete life, is a possibility for only a few; Aristotle's ethic becomes elitist.[22]

One way out of this dilemma is to see that even though Aristotle describes virtue friendships as perfect, this does not mean the friends themselves are perfectly virtuous. Aristotle calls these relationships perfect not so much because of the qualities of the friends, though it is partly that, but more exactly because of the moral possibilities of the friendship. These relationships promise a possibility for growth in virtue and character that outside such relationships would not be possible. Aristotle calls our attention not to the friends, but to the power of the relationship. As Cooper points out, "On Aristotle's theory what makes a friendship a virtue-friendship is the binding force within it of some—perhaps, for all that, partial and incomplete—excellence of character,"[23] but the fact that the virtue of each is incomplete is the very reason they are drawn to and need the friendship of one another. It is in the activity of virtue friendships that the good qualities we have are developed and enhanced. Friendships of character and virtue are perfect not because the friends are, but because we cannot have the moral life without them.

A second question Cooper raises to Aristotle's claim that only friendships based on moral goodness are friendships truly is whether the other two types of friendship, friendships of usefulness and of pleasure, are so lacking that they cannot satisfy the requirements of friendship at all. Cooper notes that Aristotle defines friendship in general as "mutual well-wishing out of concern for one another; he makes it characteristic of friendships, of whatever type, that a friend wishes well to his friend for his friend's own sake."[24] Are friendships of usefulness and pleasure, which are clearly also part of our life, so motivated by self-seeking that they can never count as friendships? Aristotle sometimes gives this impression. Even though he defines friendship in general before specifying its three types, thus implying "that not only in 'perfect' friendship but also in pleasure—and advantage—friendship a friend wishes his friend well for the friend's own sake,"[25] Cooper notes that

> on the other hand, Aristotle repeatedly contrasts the two derivative types of friendship with the basic type by emphasizing the self-centeredness of pleasure—and advantage—friends; thus he says that in erotic relationships (one class of pleasure-

friendships) people 'love not one another but their incidental features' (1164a10–12), that is, what gives pleasure to themselves. . . . This seems to suggest that in pleasure—and advantage—friendships each party is concerned solely with his own good, and this would mean that they could not have the sort of concern for one another that Aristotle seems in 8.2 to attribute to friends.[26]

Are these two kinds of friendship purely exploitative? A careful reading of Aristotle indicates they are not. Though describing them as friendships only incidentally and not essentially, Aristotle nonetheless counts them as kinds of friendships. As Cooper puts it, if Aristotle sees friendship "as always involving well-wishing to one's friend for his own sake, then the types will have much in common: in every friendship, of whichever of the three types, the friend will wish his friend whatever is good, for his own sake, and it will be mutually known to them that this well-wishing is reciprocated."[27]

Martha C. Nussbaum agrees. In her book, *The Fragility of Goodness,* Nussbaum notes that the three types of friendship are distinguished not in terms of their objects and goals, which are always the other person and his or her well-being, but in terms of the basis or ground of the friendship, which will be pleasure in some cases, advantage in others, and good character in still more. "Pleasure, advantage, and good character are three different bases or original grounds of philia; they are not the goal or final (intentional) end of the relationship," Nussbaum writes. "In other words, the two people are friends 'through' or 'on the basis of' these, but the goal they try to achieve in action will still be some sort of mutual benefit."[28] This is why friendships of pleasure and usefulness, though not perfect, are still not exploitative. They would be exploitative if each person aimed solely at his or her own pleasure or advantage, and not at that of the friend; however, if that were the case they would not be friendships at all. As Nussbaum says about friendships of pleasure or usefulness, "Such relationships will not be merely exploitative: for we recall that without mutuality of genuine well-wishing for the other person's own sake the relationship will not deserve the title of philia at all. There can be genuinely disinterested mutual benefit in cases where the basis of attachment is shallow and partial. Business partners may give one another gifts and entertain one another; young lovers, knowing only one another's pleasantness, may still genuinely contribute, unselfishly, to one another's good."[29]

Though not ideal and certainly not sufficient for eudaimonia, these most common friendships of usefulness and pleasure have positive value. The fact that Aristotle delineates three kinds of friendship suggests each human life needs to include all three. While it is true that of the three, character friendships are most important, it is also true that not every friendship needs to be or even can be of this type; not every friendship could sustain the intensity and rigor virtue friendships require.

Each type of friendship is good because each contributes to our well-being and is an element in a fulsome life, but friendships based on moral goodness are better, because of what they can do for the friends. These friendships make people good, and their usefulness is precisely the virtue they mediate to the friends. In this sense, there is no friendship more useful or advantageous than character friendships for it is these relationships which bring men and women to the goodness in which human fullness consists. Thus, what sets virtue friendships apart from other friendships is not the way one friend beholds the other, but the substance of the friendship itself. Friendships formed from virtue have greater moral possibilities than friendships formed from usefulness or pleasure. Each ought to be part of every human life, but friendships of virtue are friendships in the best sense because no one can be good, and therefore human, without them.

What leads Aristotle to this high evaluation of friendship

is his persistent inquiry into the ingredients of a flourishing life. The *Nichomachean Ethics* represents Aristotle's answer to what a complete life, a life capable of eudaimonia, would be. It is this pressing search to understand and delineate human flourishing that leads Aristotle to friendship: for him one cannot have a good life without it. The value of having friends is best disclosed when we consider how we would proceed if we were to design for ourselves the best possible human life. Whatever else such a life would include, it would necessarily include friends.[30]

In his essay, "Aristotle on Friendship," which is cited extensively in this section because it is the best among the scant literature on this subject, Cooper lists several reasons why Aristotle says we seek the company of friends and could not consider our life complete without them. First, friendship is an important source of self-awareness and self-understanding. Each of us wants to know ourself, we wish to come to an honest appraisal of who we are, but Aristotle knew this knowledge of self often comes not directly, but through our friends. Why is this?

In virtue friendships each person is attracted to the other because they sense in one another a similarity of character, a kinship in goodness. We are drawn to certain people because of a compatibility in values and principles we sense with them, because at least intuitively we feel an agreement with them on what we consider important, an agreement on our estimate of the point and purpose of life. True, to be our friends they must be other—there must be something uniquely different about them to sustain a relationship—but there must also be a similarity in ideals and values, what Cooper calls a "strong underlying similarity of character and views" that is "intuitively felt by each in the other" if there is to be friendship at all.[31] This similarity in goodness enables self-knowledge. If a person knows he is like his friend in goodness, then by coming to know his friend he comes to know himself.

The friend is like a mirror. We can consider ourselves

directly, but often we see ourselves better through one who is like us, for then we see ourselves reflected in one who is a "mirror image" of our goodness.[32] Aristotle notes that a friend is "another self," and he takes this very seriously. We do think of our friends as "another self" because of all we share in common with them. The value of these friendships is that they offer us an objective knowledge of ourselves. "The claim, here again," Cooper writes, "seems to be that it is only or best in character-friendship that one can come to know oneself—to know the objective quality of one's own actions, character, and life."[33]

> For knowing intuitively that he and his friend are alike in character, such a person could, by studying his friend's character, come to know his own. Here the presumption is that even an intimate friend remains distinct enough to be studied objectively; yet because one intuitively knows oneself to be fundamentally the same in character as he is, one obtains through him an objective view of oneself. In the MM's [*Magna Moralia*] image, one recognizes the quality of one's own character and one's own life by seeing it reflected, as in a mirror, in one's friend.[34]

A second reason for the value of friendship is simply that friends protect us from the boredom to which even the most important and interesting activities are prone. No matter how worthwhile an activity may be, if we are forced to pursue it by ourselves we will likely tire of it. We tire of our projects not because their value lessens, but because left to ourselves we are incapable of appreciating what their value is; we require others in order to learn why the projects and concerns of our life actually are so important to us.[35]

This is especially crucial when those activities and interests are the virtuous life. If eudaimonia is life understood as the pursuit of virtue, the ability to remain engaged with the virtuous life is absolutely essential. One cannot afford to tire of virtue because to become disengaged with its activities is to begin a deterioration of self no one can long endure. Friendship is especially crucial because without the support and reassurance of others who are involved with us in the virtuous life, we invariably grow disenchanted with the very activities we cannot afford to doubt. As Cooper comments,

> It is clear enough, however, that the satisfactions that derive from shared activity are especially needed in connection with those activities, whatever they may be, that are most central to a person's life and contribute most decisively to his flourishing, as he himself conceives it. For here the flagging of one's commitments and interests will be particularly debilitating; here more than anywhere else one needs the confirmatory sense that others too share one's convictions about which activities are worthwhile, and the other benefits of sharing pointed out above. Now on Aristotle's theory of eudaimonia the flourishing human life consists essentially of morally and intellectually excellent activities. So the flourishing person will have a special need to share these activities, if his own interests in life are to be securely and deeply anchored. . . . Hence, a human being cannot have a flourishing life except by having intimate friends to whom he is attached precisely on account of their good qualities of character and who are similarly attached to him: it is only with such persons that he can share the moral activities that are most central to his life.[36]

We need this reassurance that others care about what we do. It is their commitment to the same causes or projects that convinces us that those things to which we have given our life are truly worth our life. Our life's activity is enhanced for us when we can be engaged in it with others, because with and through them we learn how varied and rich are the goods the activity promises. That the activity's good cannot be exhausted by ourselves, but is uniquely and variously displayed by others, is further evidence of its worth. "It seems not unreasonable to suggest, then," Cooper says, "that the sort of confirmation of the worth of one's endeavors and pursuits which is so valuable, perhaps necessary, to a human being if he is to sustain his interests is hardly available outside of the context of a shared activity."[37] We need friendships formed from shared purposes, friendships whose activity is the mutual pursuit and embodiment of those purposes, if we are not to become disinterested with the projects upon which the self depends.[38]

A third reason for why we seek the company of friends is that when we share activities with others we are able to be involved in those activities much more extensively than we could be if those activities were private. Cooper says we can be involved in an activity in two ways, either directly or indirectly. Obviously our participation is greater if we are directly and immediately involved; however, if the activity is shared, there is a sense of being involved even if at a particular moment we are not directly engaged in the activity itself. The fact that others participate in the same activity extends our sense of participation, enabling us to feel kinship with them even though we may not actually be involved with them.

A perfect example of this is the virtuous life. We are directly involved in the life of virtue when we are engaged in virtuous activity ourselves. But we are also indirectly involved in the life of virtue anytime anyone who shares our commitment to virtue is engaged by it. The nature of joint activities is that they enlarge possibilities for participation. If an activity is purely solitary, there is no participation beyond our own direct and immediate involvement; however, if the activity is shared, if it is something we seek in the company of friends, then there is a way in which we share in their pursuit and cultivation of virtue even when we are not directly involved; the fact that their primary life activity is also our own enables this kinship and connectedness.[39]

A fourth and most important reason we seek the company of friends, though implicit in Cooper's study,[40] needs to be noted explicitly: We cannot become good without them. When Aristotle begins his analysis of friendship in Book

VIII of the *Nichomachean Ethics,* he says friendship "is some sort of excellence or virtue, or involves virtue, and it is, moreover, most indispensable for life."[41] One has the feeling Aristotle is not yet clear how friendship functions in the moral life, whether it is a single virtue or a context for acquiring and exercising the virtues; and yet, he is sure friendship and virtue are connected, and somehow friendship is integral to the moral life. By the end of Book IX, however, Aristotle's appreciation of friendship has deepened. Here he says, "We may also get some sort of training in virtue or excellence from living together with good men, as Theognis says."[42]

Now the argument is much stronger. Friendship stands not just as a single virtue, but also as the relationship by which people become good; it appears as exactly the activity in which we are trained and tutored in the virtues. By spending time together with people who are good, by sharing and delighting with them in our mutual love for the good, we are more fully impressed with the good ourselves. By the end of Book IX of the *Nichomachean Ethics,* Aristotle's notion of friendship has developed to where it stands as the ongoing life activity in which the virtues are acquired and celebrated. Friendship is not just a relationship, it is a moral enterprise. People spend their lives together doing good because that is what they see their lives to be.[43]

In Book VIII and Book IX of the *Nichomachean Ethics* an argument has been building. Early in his discussion of friendship, Aristotle says friends are bound together by something they share in common.[44] It is some common interest, some shared value or delight, that attracts people and gives them a reason to become friends. For friendships of pleasure and usefulness it is one thing, maybe drinking together, maybe playing dice; but for friendships of virtue it is a shared love for what is good, a common desire to grow in virtue, to achieve one's fullness in goodness. When Aristotle discusses the common bond in which friendship begins and the deepening of which is its life, he says, "And the proverb 'friends hold in common what they have' is correct, for friendship consists in community."[45]

What is Aristotle telling us? The bond in character friendship is a love for virtue, but this is no impersonal, abstract good; rather, it is an embodied good, a good friends see taken to heart and enfleshed in the life of another. What attracts us to our friends is exactly how the good has taken root in them. Furthermore, when Aristotle says friendship "consists in community," in character friendships it is a community of virtue, a relationship or set of relationships defined by the purpose from which it began and for which it continues, the ongoing growth of each friend in the good that is her life. In this way, friendship is the community of those who seek and delight in virtue, but as a community it is not just a relationship, but a moral activity. Indeed, friendship is the activity of acquiring and growing in the virtues, a community whose purpose is its constitutive activity, namely, to be the relationship in which those who love the good actually become good.

In Book IX Aristotle forges a tighter connection between friendship and eudaimonia. He begins his argument by addressing an objection: "It has been said that supremely happy and self-sufficient people do not need friends, since they already have the good things of life. Therefore, it is argued, since they are self-sufficient, they have no need of anything further; we need a friend, who is another self, only to provide what we are unable to provide by ourselves; hence the verse: 'When fortune smiles, what need is there of friends?'"[46]

Aristotle begins his response by addressing experience. He comments that it would seem strange "to assign all good things to a happy man without attributing friends to him, who are thought to be the greatest of external goods."[47] It is impossible for Aristotle to conceive of the perfect and complete life without friends, and he presumes it would be impossible for us as well. Whatever else may comprise the best of all possible lives, all would agree friendship would be part of it.

But why? Here Aristotle's argument comes into full view. He grants that we need friends "only to provide what we are unable to provide by ourselves," but then argues that is exactly the point. The one thing we cannot provide by ourselves is virtue. Aristotle is ruggedly pragmatic about this. Virtue cannot be attained in solitude. By definition it *is* relationship because the virtuous life is the activity of doing good, of practicing good, of developing good habits; and as such, it needs opportunities to be exercised, it demands others on whom the good can be bestowed. As Aristotle puts it, "Also, if the function of a friend is to do good rather than to be treated well, if the performance of good deeds is the mark of a good man and of excellence, and if it is nobler to do good to a friend than to a stranger, then a man of high moral standards will need people to whom he can do good."[48]

This is where the connection between friendship and eudaimonia is made. Eudaimonia is life lived according to virtue, but to live according to virtue is to live in the company of friends. Friendship is a practical implication of what the moral life requires. Aristotle has already told us that eudaimonia describes the complete and fulsome life, and he has identified eudaimonia as the life of virtue, the ongoing growth of a person in goodness. Now Aristotle inquires into what training in virtue involves, and sees it centered in friendship. He bases this conclusion on his earlier argument that "happiness is some kind of activity,"[49] specifically the activity of virtue, and now suggests that since the "activity of a good man" is the doing of good with and for others, "it follows that a supremely happy man will need friends of this kind."[50] In other words, eudaimonia is life constituted by virtue friendships.

One question we will address in the final chapter is how

those within these communities of friendship relate to those
outside them; that is, does justice require that the acquisition of virtue be measured by the presence or absence in the
friends of hospitality to others? For now it is enough to
appreciate the argument Aristotle has advanced. In the beginning of his *Nichomachean Ethics,* Aristotle connects the
moral life with the purpose or telos every human life is
meant to achieve insofar as it can claim to be a human life.
This purpose is mediated through the virtues, that is why
Aristotle insists on connecting eudaimonia to the virtuous
life. At this point, Aristotle still links the moral life to the
polis. But with the city-state's loss of commitment to the
life of virtue, Aristotle is dogged by the question of how
the virtues can be acquired and how through them we can
come in touch with our good. He finds the answer in
friendship. In his analysis of the role of friendship in the
moral life Aristotle realizes we need friends not only to be
the recipients of our virtuous acts, but, more profoundly,
we also need them as the people in company with whom
we are continually formed in the good.

Acquiring virtue requires something more than just another person who becomes the occasion of our kindness, for
if that were the case we would really not need friends,
anyone would do. We need not only someone to whom to
do good, we need the community of those whose lives mean
for them what life means for us. Aristotle suggests that if
life is essentially a group project, eudaimonia is too. Aristotle says friendship in general requires that "whatever each
group of people loves most in life, in that activity they
spend their days together. For since they wish to live together with their friends, they follow and share in those
pursuits which, they think, constitute their life together."[51] Eudaimonia, specifically, is the group activity
of the virtuous life, understanding that to constitute not
just the life of each member singly, but the life of all
together. The happiness and well-being of each is this ongo-

ing collective nurturing of the good. The interconnection between the virtues and eudaimonia and friendship demands that happiness is always a group affair.

And so Aristotle is saying much more than that friendship makes the virtues more interesting and pleasant; he says friendship makes the life of virtue *possible*. Everyone seeking to become good has to discover how she or he comes in touch with the good. In the case of virtue, it comes through ongoing relationships with those who share that love. None of us can achieve eudaimonia alone, and we will be perpetually frustrated if we reach for it directly. No, eudaimonia is the gift of the other's friendship. Goodness is not aimed at directly, it is mediated through the love exchanged among friends. It is this mutual, communal seeking of the good that makes us good. But even more than that, in this mutual, communal seeking of the good we make one another good. In a way, it is more correct to say that our friends make us good, for it is in this activity of sharing the good that each of us, in his or her love for that good, becomes a source for the other person's goodness.

This makes Aristotle's description of friends as those who work for the good of the other for the other's sake even more powerful; indeed, it is through such a collective desire to live for the good of the other that each of us becomes the good we seek. Aristotle touches this when he says in virtue friendships the good "become better as they are active together and correct one another: from the mould of the other each takes the imprint of the traits he likes, whence the saying: 'Noble things from noble people'."[52] Thus, friendship is the constitutive activity of the moral life because it describes those ongoing relationships born from a love of virtue, whereby those who are devoted to the good participate in the good and, by seeking it for one another and sharing it among one another, are transfigured in goodness themselves.

This seems a long way from *Love in the Ruins*, but actually Aristotle provides what Walker Percy knows must be retrieved if the puzzled people of Paradise Estates are ever to learn why, in the best of all worlds, they are strangely unhappy. Early in that novel there is a scene in which Charley Parker, the Paradise Estates golf pro, goes to see Dr. Thomas More. "In the physical," the doctor notes, "he checked out well in all categories, being indeed a superb physical specimen as well as a genial outgoing sort of fellow." Yet "healthy as he was, and with every reason to be happy," Dr. Thomas More observes, "Charley's deep pineal, the site of inner selfhood, was barely ticking over at a miserable 0.1 mmv."[53] To discover why, the doctor gets Charley talking. After ticking off all the assets of his life, all the obvious reasons why everything should be okay, Charley admits, "'I mean like this morning I looked at myself in the mirror and I said, Charley, who in the hell are you? What does it all mean? It was strange, Doc. What does it all mean, is the thing.'"[54]

As audacious as it sounds, every moral system worthy of attention has to tackle that question. Percy is right, "What does it all mean, is the thing," and that is what Aristotle tried to figure out. In *Love in the Ruins* this best of all possible worlds is broken down the middle "because the center did not hold." That center was the conviction that life has a purpose and the meaning of being human is not only to discover that purpose, but to live according to it. For Aristotle this means understanding our life to be a transformation of the self in the good. It means a hunger for fullness and completion that cannot be had apart from virtue. It means the achievement of this fullness, not in isolation, but in community with those who share that same love and understand their life to be the never-ending activity of seeking it. This is "what it all means" for Aristotle. He refused to separate the fullness of human life from the special purpose given men and women to achieve. For him, morality was a matter of discovering and making good on this purpose. Like the people of Paradise Estates, Aristotle agrees everyone wants to be happy, it is the great longing with which we are born and with which we die. But unlike those people, Aristotle's happiness had a moral meaning. Happiness, what Aristotle called eudaimonia, was life lived according to virtue. As the *Nichomachean Ethics* developed, Aristotle learned eudaimonia and virtue had to be connected with friendship; indeed, eudaimonia became for him the community of friendship of those who are good, because he realized we only come in touch with the good when we seek and share it with others.

And maybe in this respect the world of *Love in the Ruins* is not so far from Athens after all. Aristotle makes the friendship of people who are good the center and preserve of the moral life because in the city-state at-large he sees not this commitment to virtue, but the perilous and alarming chaos of everyone becoming a law unto themselves. If the city-state is to survive and the moral life be sustained, there must be these smaller communities, these numerically humble but morally powerful enclaves of virtue, in which a commitment to the good abides. Aristotle called these friendships not just any friendships, but the friendships of those who love virtue. In the *Nichomachean Ethics* they emerge as central to the moral life not only because they become the context in which the moral life survives, but also because in them lives a hope the world too easily forgets it needs.

Similarly, in *Love in the Ruins,* the "city-state" of Paradise Estates is imperiled because "the channels are jammed and the word is not getting through."[55] But hope abides there too in another, much smaller, community of virtue— that ragtag bunch that gathers each Sunday to hear and receive the Word. "They're an odd lot, a remnant of a remnant, bits and pieces, leftovers, like the strays and stragglers after a battle,"[56] Percy tells us, but Paradise Estates cannot get on without them. Through this overlooked community of friends, a community having nothing more in common than the Word they share between them, a world that otherwise has lost its center lives by a hope it has not yet learned to make its own. We are talking about the Christian community, the church, a people pledged to practice the love of a God who embraces all. Is such a love compatible with friendship? How the Christian tradition has understood this love to relate to friendship is discussed in the next chapter.

4. Friendship as Preferential Love:

Can It Be Justified?

I. Why Friendship Pales as Christian Love

Friendship may always have been part of Aristotle's world, but it has not always been snugly at home in the Christian world. Though this seems odd to people who count their life blessed in their friends, friendship has had a difficult time justifying itself as Christian love. As Gilbert C. Meilaender says so well, "Within Christian thought agape [Christian love] displaced philia [friendship], and it is impossible to think theologically about love without giving that simple fact careful consideration."[1]

Agape puts friendship on the fringe[2] because friendship is preferential love. To have a friend is to prefer one over others, a selective love based on an attraction we feel for some but do not feel for all. That is why agape is impatient with friendship. Agape, the distinctive Christian love, is not preferential, but universal. It is a love restricted to no one and open to everyone. When we hold both loves up side-by-side, what do we see? In friendship we see an exclusive, preferential, reciprocal love based on what people find attractive in one another. In agape we see an inclusive, universal love that goes out to anyone regardless of whether that love is returned, regardless of whether we find the person easy to love or not. "Philia is clearly a preferential bond in which we are drawn by what is attractive or choice-worthy in the friend; agape is to be nonpreferential, like the

70

love of the Father in heaven who makes his sun rise on the evil and the good and sends rain on the just and the unjust (Matthew 5:45)," Meilaender explains. "Philia is, in addition, a mutual bond, marked by the inner reciprocities of love; agape is to be shown even to the enemy, who, of course, cannot be expected to return such love. Philia is recognized to be subject to change; agape is to be characterized by the same fidelity which God shows to his covenant."[3]

Given this description of friendship and Christian love, it is not surprising that at best their relationship is often seen to be problematic, at worst irreconcilable. The Gordian knot is this element of preference. Once agape is designated the love proper to Christianity and defined as both unconditional and universal, friendship, despite whatever Christian garb in which we may dress it, will be assessed a lesser, secondary love that intrinsically fails what Christian love requires. We may protest with Aristotle and Cicero and Aelred of Rievaulx that no life can be declared good without it, but our protests will have the wearying effect of leaving us further from the love we are called to satisfy. As Meilaender reminds us, "When the streams of classical thought about friendship and the Christian teaching of agape flow together, the ideal of particular friendship becomes haunted by the requirement of universal love."[4] This does not mean friendship is bad, but it does mean that from a Christian perspective it is lacking. Friendship is a necessary good in any life, but it is not a specifically Christian good. It is a powerful love, but it is not the love by which we imitate Christ. Given the relationship between agape and philia, to begin to be friends is not to begin to be Christian. Friendship is one life, agape another. Friendship is good love, but it is not redemptive love, and that explains why the relationship between philia and agape, even if not inalterably conflictual, is inalterably strained.

However, the problem may not be with friendship, but in how its relationship to Christian love has often been construed. No matter how well an apology for friendship might be made, it could never satisfy agape's demands because two things were assumed. First, it was assumed agape and philia were independent and complete in themselves, that is, one was not only defined independently of the other, but could be understood without reference to the other. In this way, it was presumed that there was no intrinsic connection between friendship and Christian love, and that each could be given full definition apart from the other; in fact, it was precisely in agape being something other than philia, and vice versa, that each was rightly understood. Once the relationship between them was thus construed, no matter how the merits of friendship might be extolled, it could never be embraced by agape. Their relationship had to be tensive because the intelligibility of each was secured by one being defined against the other.

Secondly, agape and philia were destined to be at odds because friendships (as well as agape) were viewed too abstractly. Agape was the love which made one like God, but that description was seldom applied to friendship because it was forgotten that friendship is not an abstraction, but a way of life based upon a tradition. What shape a friendship takes, what it achieves and what becomes of it, depends on what friends take the purpose of their friendship to be. In the language of contemporary ethics, understanding friendship requires understanding the narrative or story in which it is situated and according to which it is explained.[5] That is why friendships mean nothing in themselves. To understand a friendship we must ask, "A friendship for what?" There is no such thing as friendship simply, friendship pried free of a tradition, because every friendship is a relationship in which persons with and through one another try to achieve that tradition's good.

For instance, both Aristotle and Aquinas talk of friendship, but what they mean by it and how it functions are quite different. What friendship sets out to achieve is one thing if the friends aim to secure excellence in Athens, another thing if they aim for the Kingdom of God. Part of the reason philia is so often overruled by agape is that it is interpreted apart from the narrative that allows it to be integral to the Christian life. Similarly, part of the reason agape seems so remote from the everyday life of friendship is that it, too, is viewed so abstractly, lifted out of the relationships which make agape real. Some accounts of friendship may indeed be inimical to Christian love, but that is not necessarily friendship's liability, but a weakness of the narrative according to which it is judged. On the other hand, friendship both born from and seeking the Kingdom may be exactly the kind of love which enables us ultimately to be friends of the world. In that case, we do not leave preferential love behind, we extend its domain. In short, if we are rightly to understand and evaluate friendship alongside agape, we must first note the narrative which forms the lives of the friends. In doing so we may discover what leaves philia in tension with agape is not that the former is preferential and the latter is not, for agape may be nothing more than learning to love the people God loves; rather, the tension may come from a friendship which seeks something other than the Kingdom of God.

If friendship is to be a model for the moral life, especially the Christian moral life, it must take seriously the charge that Christian love, if not directly opposed to friendship, finally leaves it behind. If that is so, friendship, despite all its appeal, can hardly be offered as a way to pursue the Gospel life. In this chapter we shall argue whether or not friendship is at odds with agape depends not on the nature of friendship itself, but on the narrative by which it is formed. It may be that when friendship is not left an abstraction but is qualified by the Christian narrative, the relationship between friendship and agape is no longer problematic. It may also be that agape cannot be learned apart from those Christian friendships in which we are taught rightly how to love.

Moreover, we shall suggest that neither philia nor agape

can be defined apart from the other; not only is agape learned in Christian friendship, agape is a kind of friendship extended to the world, to those whom Jesus called our neighbors, even if those neighbors be our foes. Philia and agape are not only compatible, they are internally connected. That is why agape does not replace friendship, it is what friendship born from charity becomes. Any friendship bonded by a love that seeks first the Kingdom of God explodes into a friendship for a humanity for whom the Kingdom rightly is home. Agape is an outgrowth of philia when philia is a bonding in caritas. In this way, agape is not a love that leaves friendship behind, but a love which describes the ever-widening scope of a friendship whose members are trying to be like God. With agape we come, like God, to make friends with the world.

Before we show how this might be true, we must examine carefully the arguments of those who say friendship and Christian love must forever be opposed, for it is only in understanding their position, and learning from it, that we can appreciate how finely the relationship between philia and agape must be explored if our claim about their status can be maintained. Soren Kierkegaard and Anders Nygren are two who claimed agape leaves preferential loves behind, and it is their arguments we shall first examine.

II. How Christian Love Thrusts Friendship Aside

Soren Kierkegaard

Kierkegaard leaves little doubt about what agape does to friendship. He does not look at friendship directly, he looks at it in light of agape, and it is a scrutiny friendship cannot endure. It is not just that agape is a better love than friendship, it is so undeniably superior that its presence is a judgment on a lesser love; in the presence of agape we see defects in friendship we had not noticed before.

In Kierkegaard's mind, friendship and Christian love are not only essentially different, they are radically opposed. One cannot endure the other. It is a question of making choices, of deciding which love will be ours. We cannot have both philia and agape, we cannot give each a portion of our lives. If we choose to make friendship the love of our life, the love that makes us like God will stand eternally out of reach. If we choose to model our love on God, we shall abandon friendship for the love Jesus commanded must be ours. For Kierkegaard, agape and philia exist in such extreme tension they can never co-exist. The power of agape is that it teaches us every person is our neighbor and we are called to love them all, but it teaches us this not by enlarging our friendships, but by abandoning them. Early in *Works of Love,* Kierkegaard explains:

> One should rather take pains to clarify the point of contention in order calmly to admit in the defence that Christianity has thrust erotic love and friendship from the throne, the love rooted in mood and inclination, preferential love, in order to establish spiritual love in its place, love to one's neighbour, a love which in all earnestness and truth is inwardly more tender in the union of two persons than erotic love is and more faithful in the sincerity of close relationship than the most famous friendship. One must rather take pains to make very clear that the praise of erotic love and friendship belong to paganism, that the poet really belongs to paganism since his task belongs to it—in order with the sure spirit of conviction to give to Christianity what belongs to Christianity, love to one's neighbor, of which not a trace is found in paganism.[6]

Friendship and agape move in opposite directions. Friendship is erotic, based on attraction; agape is spiritual, based on God's command. Friendship is fickle, agape is faithful. Friendship is preferential, and therefore selfish; agape is inclusive, and therefore more generous. Friendship receives the highest praise of the pagans, for that is the kind of love it is, but for Christians friendship is a love that has to be scorned. This is the picture Kierkegaard draws, succinctly, sharply, two loves in such antithesis there is no point of contact, no smidgen of similarity between them. They are loves which inhabit different worlds: the world of friendship is pagan, the world of agape is Christian. The world of friendship is known by its exclusivity and jealousy and possessiveness, while agape is a world without boundary, choice, or distinction. Friendship is a small world in which only a few belong; agape is a world which knows no outsider. "Christian love teaches love of all men," Kierkegaard writes. "Just as decidedly as erotic love strains in the direction of the one and only beloved, just as decidedly and powerfully does Christian love press in the opposite direction."[7] And not surprisingly, the root of this animosity is friendship's basis in preference. For Kierkegaard it is friendship's Achilles' heel, the formal quality which vitiates anything else about this love that might possibly make it good. To have friendship, says Kierkegaard, is automatically to love some instead of others, and once that is the case we stand on something other than Christian terrain. A love born of preference, friendship stands forever outside agape's world.[8]

Preference locks friendship in a selfishness from which it can never escape, as Kierkegaard sees it. Friendship is a love ruined from the start because its formal quality, preference, is something Christian love can never have. No amount of subsequent achievement can extricate friendship from such ignoble beginnings. For Kierkegaard, its roots in preference make friendship nothing more than an elaborate form of self-love. To choose one over another is to seek a benefit for the self; thus, friendship is selfishness. To be deceived by friendship is to forget the grasping spirit from which it began. "Consequently Christianity has misgivings about erotic love and friendship," Kierkegaard explains, "because preference in passion or passionate preference is really another form of self-love. . . . Therefore what paganism called love, in contrast to self-love, was preference. But if passionate preference is essentially another form of self-love, one again sees the truth in the saying of the worthy father, 'The virtues of paganism are glittering vices'."[9]

Kierkegaard takes the classic description of a friend as "another self" and turns it on its head. It is proof, he argues, not of friendship's nobility, but of its selfishness. In friendship, we love the other not for his or her sake, not for the goodness we see in them, not even for their individuality or uniqueness, but we love them as "another I," a reflection and extension of ourselves. In this respect, to speak of the friend as "another self" is further testimony of the ego's penchant to establish hegemony wherever it can. As Kierkegaard puts it, "The beloved and the friend are therefore called, remarkably and significantly enough, the other-self, the other-I. . . . But wherein lies self-love? It lies in the I, in the self. Would not self-love, then, still remain in loving the other self, the other-I?"[10]

Kierkegaard emphatically answers yes. Friendship is selfishness disguised. Because we love the friend not for who he or she truly is, but only insofar as we can see in them ourselves, the deeper our love for a friend, the deeper our absorption in ourselves; the greater our devotion to a friend, the greater our obsession with ourselves. Given the delusion under which every friendship operates for Kierkegaard, the irony, as well as the tragedy of friendship, is that the greater the union in love we think we have with our friends, the greater the imprisonment we have within ourselves. What appears to the pagans to be the best of friendships every Christian recognizes to be an intoxicating infatuation with the self. Every Christian knows friendship is not just lacking, it is the most exorbitant and shameless form of self-love; it is the apotheosis of the endless human attempt at self-deification. In a disturbing passage, Kierkegaard summarizes,

> Love and friendship are the very height of self-feeling, the I intoxicated in the other-I. The more securely the two I's come

together to become one I, the more this united I selfishly cuts itself off from all others. At the peak of love and friendship the two really become one self, one I. This is explainable only because in this exclusive love there are natural determinants (tendencies, inclinations) and self-love, which selfishly can unite the two in a new selfish self. . . . In love and friendship one's neighbour is not loved but one's other-self, or the first I once again, but more intensely. . . . If anyone thinks that by falling in love or by finding a friend he has learned Christian love, he is in profound error. . . . [T]he beloved whom he loves as himself is not his neighbour; the beloved is his other-I. Whether we talk of the first-I or the other-I, we do not come a step closer to one's neighbour, for one's neighbour is the first-Thou. The one whom self-love in the strictest sense loves is also basically the other-I, for the other-I is oneself, and this is indeed self-love. In the same way it is self-love to love the other-I which is the beloved or the friend. Just as self-love in the strictest sense has been characterised as self-deification, so love and friendship (as the poet understands it, and with his understanding this love stands and falls) are essentially idolatry.[11]

What is problematic in Kierkegaard's account of friendship is that he presumes so much that needs to be proven. Are these deficiencies intrinsic to friendship, or endemic to Kierkegaard's account of it? Consider the qualifiers Kierkegaard attaches to friendship: fickle, faithless, exclusive, possessive, carnal, pagan. For him friendship is an euphemism for selfishness, disguise for an inexcusable self-love.

But it is by no means clear friendship needs to be this way. *Works of Love* is an attack on all loves other than what Kierkegaard takes Christian love to be. It is a powerful, serious, often compelling attack; however, precisely because its tone is so polemical the reader is rightly suspicious. Kierkegaard wants to praise Christian love, but he praises it at the expense of every other love. He points to the excellence of agape, but so often he points indirectly; agape is superior because every other love is flawed. This is not to deny that in agape Christian love is definitively displayed, but it is to deny that agape is best grasped through a polemic against friendship. Kierkegaard establishes an antagonistic relation between friendship and agape from unwarranted assumptions about both. What needs to be asked is why we should accept Kierkegaard's account. Why should we accept that every preferential love is selfish love? Why should we accept that the essence of Christian love is self-renunciation? Or that "love to one's neighbour is . . . eternal equality in loving. . . ."?[12]

Kierkegaard rightly says friendship is preferential love, but he goes further to claim that every preferential love is exclusive, and every exclusive love is unjust. How so? A husband has, or at least ought to have, an exclusive love for his wife inasmuch as he loves his wife in preference to other women; indeed, it is just such love that keeps the marriage alive. Far from being unjust, such a preference is what justice to his wife demands. Kierkegaard presumes the preference involved in friendship necessarily leads to unjust exclusion of others. In some friendships it might. But we can also argue the best friendships are exactly the ones that make our world bigger. We can claim that the friends who genuinely love us are the ones who do not try to possess us, but the ones whose respect enables us to befriend others. At the very least, to love one in preference to another is not, as Kierkegaard implies, always to love at the expense of another. As our study of Aristotle's account of friendship demonstrated, genuine friendship is a school in virtue, a means by which people devoted to the good become good. Thus, on Aristotle's terms Kierkegaard's analysis has not undermined friendship, it has misunderstood it. If true friendship is friendship based in virtue, then what Kierkegaard has described is not friendship at all. To that extent, Aristotle would agree that the love Kierkegaard has described is morally deficient, but he would never agree that such love is friendship.

Consider Kierkegaard's claim that to love a friend "as another self" is to love the friend merely as an extension of the self. In his *Friendship, Altruism, and Morality*, Lawrence A. Blum mounts a direct challenge to Kierkegaard's claim. Like Aristotle, Blum does not deny such relationships exist, but he refuses to call them friendships. The language employed makes all the difference in coming to see what the relationship is. What Kierkegaard calls friendship is more aptly a relationship of exploitation and manipulation. If that is what it is, that is how it should be described. Relationships based on selfishness and narcissism are not friendships, they are unhealthy, disastrous relationships.

Friendships are something else. Friendship, Blum explains, "involves a high level of development and expression of the altruistic emotions of sympathy, concern, and care—a deep caring for and identification with the good of another from whom one knows oneself clearly to be other."[13] Friendship is not any relationship of preference, but one "in which one genuinely understands and knows the other person, and understands one's separateness from him."[14] Blum's language is deliberate. Friendship is preferential love, but preferential love is not necessarily selfish. If it is the preferential love of friendship, then it is a love that not only prefers the friend, but prefers the interests, concerns, and cares of the friend. As such, friendship can school us in the virtues because it demands getting outside ourself, it demands developing a horizon of interests and concerns beyond the confines of the self. Friendship enlarges the self, but only to the degree that it focuses on another precisely as other.

This is what Kierkegaard missed. He was right to critique relationships in which another was used merely as an occasion of the self's interests—such relationships can hardly be models of Christian love—but he was wrong to call them friendships. As Blum says about friendship, "For a genuine friend truly cares for the other for his own sake. He is willing to give of himself to promote the other's good; he understands the other in his own being and interests, and can distinguish the other's interests from his own, even while he is able to care deeply for their realization and in that sense identify with the friend and his good. . . . It is his human growth and happiness which he desires—and for the friend's own sake, not his own."[15] If this is what friendship is, a love which teaches caring and concern for the other, then far from being inimical to agape, it can be exactly the kind of relationship in which agape is learned. Given what Kierkegaard presumes about friendship, it can only frustrate Christian love. But if friendship is as Blum (and Aristotle) describe it, then learning to love and care for a friend can be a means of learning to love and care for many more. In this way, agape and philia are not mutually exclusive, they are intrinsically connected: friendship is the love in which agape is learned.

Oddly enough, on Kierkegaard's own terms a solution to the dichotomy he sees between friendship and Christian love can be broached. Later in *Works of Love* Kierkegaard says God must be a partner in every genuine human love. He speaks of love for God being the concern which binds people together in love, and adds that truly to love another is to help her or him seek God. Here Kierkegaard's position is more nuanced. He does not disparage special relationships of love, but says they are genuinely love only when God is the "middle term" or "third partner" who not only stands between the loved ones, but actually is the one by whom both are joined. Human love is genuine, and therefore Christian, not when it abjures preferences, but when its focus is God. Here Kierkegaard makes a qualification his earlier analysis lacked. The distinction here is not between friendship and Christian love, but between worldly love and Christian love, and what divides them is not that one is preferential and the other is not, but that the first fails to love the other in God, while the second realizes that is the only way truly to love.

> Worldly wisdom thinks that love is a relationship between man and man. Christianity teaches that love is a relationship between: man-God-man, that is, God is the middle term. However beautiful the love-relationship has been between two or more people, however complete all their enjoyment and all their bliss in mutual devotion and affection have been for them, even if all men have praised this relationship—if God and the relationship to God have been left out, then, Christianly understood, this has not been love but a mutual and enchanting illusion of love. For to love God is to love oneself in truth; to help another human being to love God is to love another man; to be helped by another human being to love God is to be loved. [16]

What is happening here? There is a modification in Kierkegaard's position, the implications of which he does not take fully into account. It is vastly different to dismiss friendship because it is preferential than to dismiss it because in such a relationship God is not a part. Thomas Aquinas, for instance, would not agree with Kierkegaard's earlier analysis, but he would find no fault with him here. In these passages Kierkegaard speaks of love relationships "between two or more people," he refers to special, particular, preferential relationships, and he blesses them insofar as God is their center. Friendship receives different evaluation here because in this instance Kierkegaard realizes the crucial question in Christian love is not that it be nonpreferential, but that its source, center, and aim be God. It is this which distinguishes Christian love from worldly love, agape from all impostors. What Kierkegaard implies is that genuine love is formally identified not by an absence of preference, but by the presence of God.

The problem with Kierkegaard's prior analysis is that he played friendship off against agape instead of relating both to the God in whom love is revealed. He made agape the norm by which friendship was to be judged, and thus overlooked the God in whom all genuine love is defined. The norm for Christian friendship is not agape, but God. Similarly, we know agape not in light of flawed friendships, but in light of the Word in whom love is unveiled. The weakness in Kierkegaard's earlier analysis was failing to see that philia and agape share the same criterion insofar as both are genuinely love to the degree they are modeled on God. In this sense, both philia and agape are secondary categories which take their meaning not in terms of one another, but in terms of the God in whom love is perfectly displayed. Once it is acknowledged that both Christian friendship and agape originate in the same love, not only are they reconcilable, they are also inseparable; that is, we not only know why agape is not opposed to friendship, we also know why it is friendship's most perfect expression.

To speak of Christian love as one in which "God is the middle term" is not to dismiss friendship, but to locate it in a different narrative, to place it in the Christian story of men and women seeking God. Once this is done friendship not only has possibilities wholly other than Kierkegaard first imagined, chief among which is a way to perfection, it also bears a vastly different description. Kierkegaard first speaks of friendship as egocentric, fickle, selfish, and erotic because he presumes it must always be pagan. He never allows God can be partner in a friendship or that God is someone friends can mutually seek. That Kierkegaard constantly describes friendship as pagan indicates the narrative to which he originally consigns it.

But friendship's possibilities change when it is relocated in the Christian story. When this occurs the fact of preference does not change, but its object does. In the Christian account, genuine friendship love demands a mutual preference for God. It is that preference, reciprocally sought and undertaken, which founds the friendship, identifies its purpose, and explains its joy. By preferring God, the friends learn what it means to prefer one another. Thus, a mistaken love is not a preferential love, but one exclusive of God. Kierkegaard admits this when he writes,

> The fundamental untruth in the merely human conception of love is that love is withdrawn from the relationship to God. . . . Everyone as an individual, before he relates himself in love to a beloved, to a friend, to lovers, to contemporaries, must first relate himself to God and the God-demand. As soon as one leaves out the God-relationship the merely human conception of what the participants wish to understand by love, what they wish to require of each other, and their mutual judgment in the power thereof become the highest judgment. [17]

When one "leaves *in* the God-relationship," what the partners understand by love and what their love requires is determined not by a human conception of love, but by God's. Thus qualified, their friendship holds forth love's grandest potential: it touches on the divine, it is a love that makes them godly. A genuine love is one that leads both persons to God. Friendship can do that, spousal love can do that, love of enemies can do that. Any love of which God is a partner, any love born from love of God, centered on God and seeking God, can do that. What makes any love Christian is that it be measured and bounded by love for God. Both friendship and agape are Christian love when they are formed according to and for the sake of God. Christian love is love modeled on the Word who is love. When that is the case, not only are friendship and agape compatible, friendship becomes the crucible in which agape is fired.

Anders Nygren

Like Kierkegaard, for Anders Nygren agape is Christianity's distinguishing mark. In his classic and pivotal work, *Agape and Eros,* Nygren says, "We have therefore every

right to say that agape is the centre of Christianity. . . .
Agape comes to us as a quite new creation of Christianity.
It sets its mark on everything in Christianity. Without it
nothing that is Christian would be Christian. Agape is
Christianity's own original basic conception."[18]

Clearly, for Nygren, to know agape is to know what it
means to be Christian. Christianity's heart and soul, agape
must be learned if Christianity is to be learned. It is what
sets Christianity apart from other religions and is that by
which Christianity is defined. Like Aquinas' claim about
charity, for Nygren agape is Christianity's formal element.
Thus, without agape all the other qualities attributed to
Christians lose their merit, they are not genuinely Christian
at all.

The resemblance to Kierkegaard is strong, for like his
Scandinavian forebear, Nygren says agape is "universal in
its scope." Other loves are "exclusive and particularistic."
Other loves set boundaries, but it is not that way with
Christian love. "Christian love . . . overleaps all such limits;
it is universal and all-embracing."[19]

How does Nygren know this? Why is he so sure this is
what agape is? He knows agape by looking to God. The
heart of Nygren's argument and the key to his methodology
is the strong connection he makes between the qualities of
agape and the qualities of God. We know agape not in itself
but derivatively, the content of agape is given in God, it is
identified through the one in whom love is wholly revealed.[20] We cannot know agape by looking at it directly.
Agape is learned by looking to God, for it is in God that
agape is definitively displayed. Put more strongly, God
does not simply reveal agape, as if this love were something
apart from God; rather, God is agape, this distinctive, redemptive love is what we learn when we come to learn
God. Although it is correct to say love is what God is, it
is more accurate to say God is what love is, for that avoids
the tendency to define the essence of love apart from the
God who perfectly is love. The problem with the former

description, Stanley Hauerwas writes, is that it is vulner-
able to the impression that "the nature of God no longer
defines the love that is his essence, but a general notion of
love tends to define his nature."[21]

But Nygren pushes this even further. He insists on the
connection between agape and God, arguing we can only
understand the former in terms of the latter, but he also
insists the knowledge of God which makes possible a
knowledge of agape is not a knowledge we can learn from
afar. We do not learn agape by thinking of God or by study
and scrutiny of the scriptures. All that is important, but it
is much too remote to bring knowledge of God and God's
love. Knowledge of God is not something gained at safe
distance, but something that comes to us by sharing in the
very life of God. As Nygren puts it, "God and Agape are
one. Agape as such, regardless of the object to which it is
directed, is participation in the life of God: Agape is born
of God."[22]

To say that "Agape is born of God" is not only to identify agape and God, but also to make agape internal to
God. If agape is internal to God, it defines the essence of
God, and if this is so it is learned by getting inside God,
by knowing God from within the life of God. Agape is
knowledge gained by participation. For Nygren, agape is
what kinship with God brings, it is a sign not of moral
astuteness, but of divine intimacy. As he puts it, "It is no
mere accident that we find here so intimate a connection
between Christian love and the Christian relationship to
God, Agape and fellowship with God. . . . There can therefore be no doubt where the starting-point is to be found
which we are seeking for our interpretation of the idea of
Agape. It is the Christian conception of fellowship with
God that gives the idea of Agape its meaning."[23]

Nygren forges this strong connection between knowing
God and knowing agape by speaking of fellowship with
God as the relationship in which agape is learned. We learn

to love as Christians should by learning to love as God does, and that knowledge comes by taking part in the life of God. It is insider's knowledge, wrought from a vulnerability to God which enables us to know God. If knowing agape demands knowing God, how do we come to know the love God is? Nygren answers that we come to know the love God is over a lifetime history of sharing in, being open to, and imitating this God. Knowing agape requires becoming godly, and we become godly inasmuch as we have shared God's life. Here Nygren is close to David Burrell's point that knowledge of God comes not prior to, but only through the kinds of practices and rituals by which we come into contact with God.[24] Nygren expresses the same by saying that "the Christian ethic is from first to last a religious ethic,"[25] a morality which cannot be learned independently of fellowship with the Divine Life.

What do we learn of agape through fellowship with God? First, we learn "Agape is spontaneous and 'unmotivated'."[26] For Nygren, "this is the most striking feature of God's love as Jesus represents it."[27] God's love is not based upon a calculation of the merits or worth of the people God loves. "We look in vain for an explanation of God's love in the character of the man who is the object of His love,"[28] and this means God's love does not balance upon our own goodness. We do not even deserve God's love, it is pure gift, prompted not by our virtue, but by the very nature of God to love.

To describe agape as spontaneous and unmotivated is to recognize that God's love is not given after God has ascertained whether there is any benefit to loving us, or if we might love God in return; nor is it measured by calculating how God's love might be rewarded with our own. No, agape means God simply loves, generously, perfectly, eternally. This first quality of agape means Christian love, like God's, must neither be determined by a calculation of possible reciprocity, nor by an assessment of the beloved's worth. As Nygren says, "It is this love, spontaneous and 'unmotivated'—having no motive outside itself, in the personal worth of men—which characterises also the action of Jesus in seeking out the lost and consorting with 'publicans and sinners'."[29] As Jesus' outpouring of love to the undeserving attests, agape is a love which is offered unconditionally. Agape's love is not contingent on the merit or goodness of the beloved; thus for Nygren the rationale for agape's love is not to be found in the loved one, but in the character of the God who loves. That agape is spontaneous and unmotivated is a reflection not of the goodness of those God loves, but of the nature of God. The absolute liberality of the Divine Love stems from the ways of God. For Nygren, the spontaneity and unmotivated character of agape is what separates it from human love. Human love is calculating and measured, God's love is unconditionally abundant.[30]

The second criterion Nygren lists for agape is closely related to the first: "Agape is 'indifferent to value'."[31] Nygren traces this aspect of agape to Jesus' treatment of sinners and outcasts. The gospels testify that Jesus kept company not with the righteous, but with sinners, with those known to break the Law. What takes place in these gospel scenes, Nygren argues, is not simply "a transvaluation, or inversion of values," as if "Jesus simply reverses the generally accepted standard of values and holds that the sinner is 'better' than the righteous." No, Nygren explains, "something of far deeper import than any 'transvaluation' is involved here—namely, the principle that any thought of valuation whatsoever is out of place in connection with fellowship with God."[32] That Jesus kept company with sinners is testimony that with God's love "all thought of valuation is excluded in advance; for if God, the Holy One, loves the sinner, it cannot be because of his sin, but in spite of his sin." By contrast, the danger of restricting God's love to the righteous is that "there is always the risk of our thinking that God loves the man on account of his righteousness and godliness. But this is a denial of Agape—as if

God's love for the 'righteous' were not just as unmotivated and spontaneous as His love for the sinner! As if there were any other Divine love than spontaneous and unmotivated Agape!"[33] Clearly, for Nygren, to understand God's love as dependent on the goodness or righteousness of a person is to misunderstand it. Where God's love is concerned, questions of the godliness of the beloved are irrelevant.

Obviously, Nygren wants to say God's love never depends on our own goodness, God simply loves, purely, generously, unconditionally. But Nygren is saying something more. He also says God never loves us in virtue of who we are, God loves us irrespective of who we are, without any consideration of what might make us lovable. Nygren pushes this stronger argument in order to exemplify the pure gratuitousness of God's love, but in doing so he breaks any connection between the quality of God's love and the quality of ourself. It is one thing to say God loves us regardless of what we do, but it is another thing to say God loves us regardless of who we are. The first underscores how the divine love persists despite our sinfulness, but the second suggests God can love us without ever taking us into account.

Nygren seems to say both. Agape is wholly a reflection of the nature of God, not at all a reflection of ourselves. To say God's love is indifferent to value is to abstract God's love from the people God loves. Positively, this indifference to value assures us God always loves, but it assures us at the cost of claiming there is no connection between why God loves and who we are. The force of these first two qualities of agape is to suggest God loves us not because of who we are, but solely because that is who God is. "It is only when all thought of the worthiness of the object is abandoned that we can understand what Agape is," Nygren writes. "God's love allows no limits to be set for it by the character or conduct of man."[34]

That is only partially consoling. If "all thought of the worthiness of the object is abandoned," then God can love us without needing to know us. Such love may be universal and unconditional, but it is also impersonal, a love that does not see our individuality. If God's love is spontaneous and unmotivated and indifferent to value as testimony that God's love is not a measure of our goodness, and that God will not abandon us when we err, that is one thing; however, if this also means God loves blindly, only because it is the nature of God to love, regardless of who we are or who we might become, then the liberality of God's love is affirmed, but the personableness of that love is lost.

We not only want God to love us, we want to love God. We want a God whose love can be returned, a God whose love enables us to be in relationship to God. If friendship is to be a model for the moral life, we must not only be the objects of that love, we must also be its partners. This does not mean we have equality with God or that we can ever love God as much or as well as God loves us, but it does mean God's love can be returned, that our love can be a response to God's, and that in this love given, received, and returned, a friendship with God can be established.

At least the possibility for such friendship with God is given in the final two criteria Nygren subscribes for agape. Agape is creative,[35] and it is "the initiator of fellowship with God."[36] By the first Nygren means it is God's love that makes us worthy of God's love. Apart from God's love, lost in sin, shut off from grace, there is nothing in us to make us lovable; however, exactly the power of God's love is its ability to bring into being what was not there before, to bestow us with a value we could never have given ourselves. For Nygren, what value we do have before God is not something we give to ourselves, nor something our own goodness could achieve, but something bestowed on us by God. Agape fashions in us the goodness which makes us lovable; thus, that we might be pleasing to God is not our achievement, but God's. For Nygren, to be loved by God is to undergo a transformation. Agape works a transfiguration in all the children of the earth, it makes worthy before

God a people who could never initiate their own restoration. To be loved by God is to suffer the transformation necessary to have fellowship with God. In this sense, human worth and goodness is not human achievement, but divine. It is the ongoing and ultimate effect of God's love on our life. As Nygren summarizes,

> Agape, is creative. God does not love that which is already in itself worthy of love, but on the contrary, that which in itself has no worth acquires worth just by becoming the object of God's love. Agape has nothing to do with the kind of love that depends on the recognition of a valuable quality in its object; Agape does not recognise value, but creates it. Agape loves, and imparts value by loving. The man who is loved by God has no value in himself; what gives him value is precisely the fact that God loves him. Agape is a value-creating principle.[37]

Secondly, to say "Agape is the initiator of fellowship with God" is to claim it is exactly the gift of God's love, the unmerited, gratuitous outpouring of God's love in our hearts, that enables us to have life with God. That we have fellowship with God is sign of God's goodness, not our own; in fact, without that gift of God's grace, life with God would be eternally beyond us. God's love is the condition for the possibility of life with God, that is why it is so purely a gift, a divine generosity on which we absolutely depend. By ourselves we could strive for fellowship with God, but we would strive in vain, for we would be grasping for a goodness utterly superior to our own.

In this respect, Nygren's claim that agape initiates fellowship with God is similar to Aquinas's claim that in order to reach God through love we first must be made 'proportionate' to God through grace. Our possibility for God depends upon a gift from God, a fact echoed in John's claim that we can only love God because God has loved us first (I John 4:10). To be redeemed we need the ongoing kinship with God by which we are healed and brought to likeness

with God. But that relationship with God, the perfection
of which is the Kingdom, is not something we can give
ourselves. It is a gift, the never-ending gesture of God to
us which allows us to respond. What agape reminds us is
that our redemption is not originally a question of how we
"could come to God," but of how God must first and
always come to us. The initiative is always with God, and
that means, Nygren says, "that there is from man's side no
way at all that leads to God. If such a thing as fellowship
between God and man nevertheless exists, this can only be
due to God's own action; God must Himself come to meet
man and offer him His fellowship. There is thus," he concludes, "no way for man to come to God, but only a way
for God to come to man: the way of Divine forgiveness,
Divine Love."[38]

Nygren's claim that "there is from man's side no way at
all that leads to God" makes sense if that refers to our
absolute dependence on God's grace. We cannot love God
without the grace that makes that response possible. Our
life with God begins in the outpouring of God's life to us.
There is no way for us to move to God without God having
first moved to us. But we want to add to Nygren's claim
that once that love has been given it needs to be returned.
We know our love to God is essentially a response to God,
but it is a response we want to make. It is both these taken
together, God's offer and our response, God's gift and our
gratitude, that constitute our return to God. We do not
return to God simply in virtue of God's love, nor simply
in virtue of our own; we return to God in and through that
ongoing relationship of a love offered and a love returned.
In other words, we return to God through friendship with
God.

It is this consideration of the qualities of agape that
governs Nygren's analysis of human love, particularly love
for the neighbor. Having shown what God's love for us is,
Nygren next asks what our love for one another should be.

Not surprisingly, he says our love for one another must conform to God's love for us. We know how to love our neighbor when we remember how God has loved us and let that love be the rule for our own. All this is consistent with Nygren's key methodological principle that our relations with one another should reflect God's relation to us. Our morality originates in our religion, which means what we ought to do for one another is taken from what God has done for us. In this way, we are not just called to love our neighbors, we are also called to love in kind, to enshrine in our love to them the agape God has shown to us. As Nygren explains, "God's Agape is the criterion of Christian love. Nothing but that which bears the impress of Agape has a right to be called Christian love. This connection between God's love and the Christian's love is clearest when the latter takes the form of neighbourly love."[39]

For Nygren then, Christian love is formally different from human love, but what makes it different is not its object, not even the extent of its generosity, but the relationship from which Christian love originates and always strives to imitate. Agape is born from God, it is love learned in fellowship with God and love striving to commemorate God. Consequently, the decisive difference between agape and any other love is a religious one. What primarily distinguishes agape is not that it is higher or better, though Nygren undoubtedly would say that it is, but that it is rooted in God and God's love, and it is from that love Christians take life. "Christian love is something other than ordinary human love," Nygren concludes. "But what gives it its special character is precisely the fact that it is patterned on God's love. There is therefore no Christian love that does not derive its character from the Agape that is found in fellowship with God."[40]

If neighbor love tries to commemorate agape, then like the Divine love it will be spontaneous, unmotivated, indifferent to value, creative, and an initiator of fellowship with

everyone, even our enemies.[41] The features of neighbor love
are derived from what we have learned of agape in fellowship with God.[42] When we consider the qualities of agape,
and thus genuine neighbor love, and hold them alongside
customary understandings of love, we glimpse how different is a love which strives to imitate God. "Measured by
the standard of Divine love, therefore, human love is not
love at all in a deeper sense, but only a form of natural
self-love, which extends its scope to embrace also benefac-
tors of the self," Nygren writes. "In distinction from this
natural love, which is displayed even by sinners, Christian
love is spontaneous and unmotivated."[43]

The echoes from Kierkegaard are pronounced. Agape is
not preferential, it is love extended to all, and it is love
motivated not by any consideration of what is lovable or
attractive in another, but solely by fidelity to God. To love
as we should is to love as God has, and for Nygren that
means to love inclusively, unconditionally, and without any
calculation of why one might be more worthy of our love
than another. To have agape is to love without exception,
it is a love that does not make choices, which offers itself
unrestrictedly to everyone because it wants to proffer to
another what it knows it has received. Agape loves without
exception because that is the love it remembers; that it is
not preferential is a sign of its indebtedness.[44]

That neighbor love, if it is to be agape, must be impar-
tial explains why Nygren has so much trouble with the
Johannine concept of love. What bothers Nygren is "the
substantial equation of neighbourly love with love for the
brethren" that he finds in John.[45] In one respect Nygren
agrees with John. If agape "is the fellowship of love," community wrought from a kinship Christians share with God,
then it is true in this community of faith there is a "depth,
warmth, and intimacy" of love "that are without parallel
elsewhere."[46]

But what Nygren also sees in his interpretation of John's

understanding of love is that "neighbourly love becomes particularistic." In John, he says, "it loses something of its original, all-embracing scope; it becomes love for those who bear the Christian name."[47] In John, Nygren fears, agape becomes preferential, there is a love alive between Christians that is different from the love they show to the world. For Nygren, the Johannine interpretation of agape weakens the account he finds in the synoptics and Paul because in John he sees a restriction of agape's embrace. There Christian love becomes both particular and preferential, it is the love the world sees at work among Christians. It is no longer spontaneous and unmotivated because it is prompted by affection for those who share the same faith. It is no longer indifferent to value because it explicitly prefers members of the community over those who stand apart. And it does not have that creative power to initiate fellowship where alienation stood before because its focus is not on the larger world, but the community of faith. For Nygren, like Kieregaard, it is exactly when agape becomes preferential that its Christian character wanes.

But like Kierkegaard, what Nygren does not see is that this community which reaches heights of love, warmth, intimacy and fellowship can, precisely because of the faith its members share in Christ, be a community that moves out to the world. There is no reason the preferential love which constitutes the community of faith entails a narrowing of its concern. As we saw with Kierkegaard, what matters is not that the love is preferential, but what the love prefers. If a community of faith is bonded together by a common endeavor to prefer the ways of God, then this preference does not impede, but actually becomes the means by which they learn to love the world. True, there is a special love among them because they see burning in another what they have come to cherish in themselves, a hunger and thirst for God, a deep desire to love God with whole heart and soul. True, they love one another in a way they do not love someone else because like Aristotle's friends, they agree on what they think important. But because their friendship is founded on this desire that is shared among them, it is also the relationship by which they learn to love the ones God has loved, the lowly, the downcast, the misbegotten, the overlooked, and even the enemy. Their love is spontaneous and unmotivated and indifferent to value and creative, and it is all this not in spite of, but because of the friendship they have in Christ.

Both Kierkegaard and Nygren offer compelling accounts of the nature of Christian love, but as we have seen, both accounts entail a presumption about special relationships, especially friendships, that does not necessarily hold. Whether their critique of friendship applies depends on the narrative understanding of friendship employed. What we have suggested is that when friendship is located not outside but within the Christian story, then far from being in opposition to agape, it is the relationship in which agape is learned and achieved. In this sense we are claiming nothing more about Christian friendships than Aristotle claimed about virtue friendships. He argued that when friends are bought together by a mutual love for the good, their friendship is a relationship in which they become good. In this way, though they are special to one another because of the love they share, precisely because of what their friendship does to them they are opened more fully to others. Similarly, we shall suggest that when friends are brought together by a mutual love for God and a desire to follow Christ, their friendship is a relationship in which they learn the ways of God, imitate Christ, and thus learn to embrace those they hitherto ignored. In this context, agape is not something other than friendship, but describes a friendship like God's, a love of such generous vision that it looks upon all men and women not as strangers but as friends. To see how this might be so, we shall look at what Augustine, Aelred of Rievaulx, and Karl Barth had to say about what it means to love both neighbor and God.

III. Friendship as a School in Christian Love

Augustine

One of Augustine's clearest statements of friendship comes in Book IV of his *Confessions*. He is thinking about the death of a dear friend, a man "sweet to me above every sweetness of that life of mine,"[48] and in this meditation considers in what genuine friendship consists. Augustine reflects that even though they had been friends from youth, sharing interests, going to school together, playing games together, and even though through the years he had grown closer to this man than to anyone else, theirs was not truly a friendship because Christ had not been its center and God had not been its goal. "But in childhood," Augustine remembers, "he was not such a friend as he became later on, and even later on ours was not a true friendship, for friendship cannot be true unless you solder it together among those who cleave to one another by the charity 'poured forth in our hearts by the Holy Spirit, who is given to us'."[49]

As Marie Aquinas McNamara points out in her excellent study, *Friendship in Saint Augustine*, with this passage Augustine Christianizes friendship.[50] He does not develop a wholly new account of friendship, for indeed Augustine's indebtedness both to Plato and Cicero is clear,[51] but situates friendship within the Christian's journey to God. McNamara notes four distinguishing marks to Augustine's understanding of friendship. First, the author and giver of friendship is God. Second, friendship must be rooted in God and seek God. Third, Christian friendship is transformed by grace. Fourth, it does not end with the Kingdom, but there reaches its perfection when everyone has perfect friendship with God.[52]

Perhaps the most intriguing aspect of Augustine's account of friendship is his insistence that we do not choose our friends, God does. Every friend is both the gift and the work of God's love. To be brought to fruition, every friendship needs the love and affection exercised between friends, but it begins not in the love they have for one another, but in the love God has for them, a love which expresses itself in the gift of their friendship. There is something quite different about this. Aristotle said it is the virtue each sees in the other that brings friends together, but Augustine says friends are brought together by God. As McNamara explains, Augustine considers friendship a "divine gift," a sign of God reaching down into our lives and actively working on our behalf. "This is the heart of Augustine's conception of friendship and his great innovation," she writes. "It is God alone who can join two persons to each other. In other words, friendship is beyond the scope of human control. One can desire to be the friend of another who is striving for perfection, but only God can effect the union."[53]

Undoubtedly this makes us look at our friends differently. We see them not as people we have selected, but as people brought into our lives by God, divine gifts in company with whom we are to seek God. As McNamara suggests, there is nothing accidental or arbitrary about these friends; on the contrary, they represent how God's redemptive love works in our lives, the concrete and personal way God chooses to draw us to the Kingdom. From first to last, these friendships are gifts. We cannot choose them, but we can receive them. We cannot control them, but we can be redeemed through them.

Second, these friendships which begin in God must be rooted in God, conformed to God, and seek God. The model and goal of the friendships is the grace from which they began, the Spirit of Love poured out into the hearts of the friends. For Augustine the only true friendship is one which originates in this outpouring of God's love, for it is only these friendships born from the Spirit that can achieve what every friendship needs to achieve, the union of the friends with God in a Kingdom of friendship with all. The friendship within God, the friendship between Father and

Son that is Spirit, is both the grace which enables genuine human friendship and the love which represents its fullness. It is according to this Trinitarian friendship that Christian friendship ought to be patterned if Kingdom friendship is to be had.[54]

For Augustine then, the friendship God is, this Trinitarian love, is the friendship from which human friendships begin, the love to which they must conform, and the community in which they are perfected. In this sense, the project of genuine human friendships is to make good on the grace from which they began, to pattern their love on God's friendship love so that this grace is brought to fullness. If, as Augustine wrote, "friendship cannot be true unless you solder it together among those who cleave to one another by the charity 'poured forth in our hearts by the Holy Spirit, who is given to us',"[55] then the bond and center of true friendship is the Spirit, it is that love which unites the friends and ought to thrive between them, and it is through that love that the friends are transformed. In this way, McNamara says, "God is the end as He is the beginning of all true friendship."[56]

Third, Christian friendship is changed by grace. As McNamara notes, it is this which gives a different substance and meaning to the friendships of those brought together by God. "It surpasses the noble pagan ideal of Cicero," McNamara explains, "where friends wish for each other the highest degree of natural virtue possible in this life; friends united by its bonds wish for each other a supernaturally virtuous life here and eternal happiness with God in heaven."[57] In both instances friendship brings goodness, but Augustine had a very distinct goodness in mind. Only friendships born from grace are genuine friendships because only in them lives the love that can bring Kingdom goodness to the friends, and thus achieve the telos for which everyone is made. What distinguishes Christian friendships from other friendships is that they are means of growing together in the love of God—that is their purpose and

rationale. All friendships are centered in the good that joins
the friends together and explains the friendship's life. Christian friendships are centered in the love of God "poured out
in our hearts," and it is growth according to this love of
God that describes best the life of the friendship. This is
why Christian friendships do not end; they deepen as the
friends draw closer to God through the love that lives between them.[58]

Friendships are to be vessels of grace, means of redemption. They are not peripheral to the Christian life, but are
relationships of conversion, in which Christians move to
God by being transfigured in their love for God. McNamara
captures well what, for Augustine, constitutes true friendship:

> First of all, agreement on human things alone does not consti-
> tute true friendship. No matter how deep the love of friends
> is for each other, their friendship will be deficient. It is only
> when agreement on things divine is added that friendship can
> be complete. . . . The neglect of divine things, therefore, does
> not permit even a partial friendship to exist. A prerequisite for
> friendship is that both persons be friends to themselves. If
> they do not love God, they are their own enemies and incapa-
> ble of friendship.[59]

The fourth characteristic of friendship McNamara culls
from Augustine is that Christian friendships reach their
perfection only in the Kingdom. This underscores the inseparable connection between Christian friendships and the
Kingdom for which they are meant to prepare us. The grace
from which the friendship begins is the fullness of life it
seeks, the perfect community in which all are perfectly
loved. For Augustine, the Kingdom is the perfection of
mutuality and benevolence that obtains when "God shall
be all in all," and it is this perfect lovelife that is both the
exemplar and goal of genuine friendship.[60]

That the measure of Christian friendship is Kingdom
love helps us understand why the preferential love of friend-

ship is not inimical to the universal love of agape, but is the context in which agape is learned. It is its origin in the Spirit of love and its culmination in the Kingdom of love that enables Christian friendship to be not an impediment, but a means to a more universal, inclusive love. As Meilaender rightly says, for Augustine these "particular friendships are to school us in love; they are a sign and a call by which God draws us toward a love more universal in scope."[61] As Meilaender understands it, God is fashioning a community, the fullness of which is the Kingdom, but that community is begun and prepared for by the friendships on earth that make men and women capable of Kingdom life because through them they have learned Kingdom love.[62] When Christians conform their friendship love to the Spirit of love, boundaries are broken, fears disappear, magnanimity reigns. In short, their friendship is preferential but not exclusive, for they welcome others to the way of life through which they will find their fullness in God. Through the preferential love of their friendship on earth, rooted as it is in Christ, they learn to prefer what God does, the perfect community of all being one in God.

This is why Meilaender speaks of these friendships as "schools of love," relationships in which Christians are tutored in the agape of Kingdom fellowship. In these preferential loves, others are not kept out but invited in, for the friends, modeling their love on the agape of God, learn to desire and seek the community of humanity with God we call Kingdom. As Meilaender explains, "Attachment to friends is a school in which we are trained for that greater community" that is the Kingdom. "Life is a journey, a pilgrimage toward that community in which friends love one another in God. . . . Along the way, friendship is a school, training us in the meaning and enactment of love."[63] Thus, what Augustine has done, Meilaender summarizes, is take the classical notion of friendship detailed by Plato, Aristotle, and Cicero and infused it with Kingdom possibilities. Preferential love is not only justified but necessary because it does not oppose agape, but teaches us what agape means.

> Elements of each of the chief classical views of friendship are taken up and transformed in Augustine's discussion. The recognition that friendship must necessarily be particular and preferential . . . finds an important place in Augustine's description of friendship. At the same time, however, these particular friendships are placed in a larger context, seen as a call toward and preparation for a love more universal in scope. And both aspects are incorporated into Augustine's theological vision. Particular friendships are justified because, in the simplest sense, God gives them to those whom he has created to live within the constraints of finitude. Particular friendships are qualified because this same God intends that they should lead us toward the love of God in which all the redeemed will share and be a school in which that love is learned. Hence, Augustine's understanding of friendship is transformed when it is placed within his vision of human life as pilgrimage.[64]

Even though Meilaender justifies the preferential love of friendship, he is not entirely comfortable with it; a tensive relationship between friendship and agape persists. Ideally, love should not be preferential but universal. That friendship is justified, as Meilaender sees it, is a concession to our status after the Fall. We need such preferential loves as the relationships which draw us to a more universal love, but this means that to the degree we learn agape, we leave friendship behind. Given our finitude and our sinfulness, friendship is the means by which fallen men and women are rehabilitated to a purer, more Godlike love; thus, friendship is justified but provisional. Growth in agape is really the evolution from a preferential love to a universal love. Thus, friendships prepare us for a love beyond friendship; indeed, its purpose is to enable us, at some point, to go on without it. As Meilaender writes, "A love like that of the Samaritan can, without denigrating the natural love of friendship given us by the Creator, move us to try to live even now as if the process by which the partial, preferential loves are transformed into nonpreferential neighbor-love were completed."[65]

McNamara interprets Augustine differently. She sees him understanding friendship not as a provisional love the Kingdom leaves behind, but an intimation of the love the Kingdom promises to be. The Kingdom marks not the end of friendship, but its perfection, it represents not a love that surpasses friendship, but friendship's fullness, the utter unity of humanity in God. As McNamara puts it, "His ideal was to have the unity which is an integral part of individual friendship reign among all men joined in fraternal charity."[66] In this way, as Christians grow in agape they do not leave their friendships behind, for the Kingdom is ultimately what their friendships become. The center of their friendships was always Christ, that is why the Kingdom represents not a different love, but an extension of the community formed by that love. This is why we can say the perfect bonding of all men and women to one another in Christ signifies not a love other than friendship, but the unity for which Christian friendship always strove. No human friendship ever wholly captures this, but insofar as it is Christian this unity is its aim. As McNamara understands it, Augustine wanted "to see Christian friendship reign among all men"[67] because that is what the Kingdom is. "In the last analysis," McNamara writes, "Augustine's ideal of perfect unity is perfect friendship among men who are joined through love inseparably to Christ, so that all together form 'the one Christ loving Himself'."[68]

The union of all men and women in Christ is the fullness of the grace from which Christian friendship began. As we noted, the task of every friendship is to bring the love of God poured out in our hearts, the Divine Friendship who is Spirit, to fullness. For friendship's grace to establish the Kingdom it intends, we must conform our lives to it and learn from it how to love one another as God has loved us; that is, we must learn to love one another as friends. In his

Commentary on the Gospel of John, McNamara notes,
Augustine writes: "'Christ has loved us that we may love
one another; the effect of His love for us is so to bind us to
one another in mutual love that we become the Body of
which He is the Head, His members linked together in
that lovely bondage'."[69] This is the Mystical Body, this
perfect union of all to one another as each is to God. That
this may someday be real, we must love everyone, even our
enemies, not just as neighbors, but as the friends in God
we are called to be.[70]

Aelred of Rievaulx

Aelred (1110–1167) was a Cistercian monk and abbot of
Rievaulx. He began writing his treatise, *Spiritual Friendship,* around 1147.[71] His dependence upon both Cicero's
De Amicitia and Augustine is clear. Like *De Amicitia,*
Aelred's treatise takes the form of a conversation among
friends. In the Prologue of *Spiritual Friendship,* Aelred acknowledges his debt to Cicero. "When I was still just a lad
at school," he tells us, "there came to my hands the treatise
which Tullius wrote on friendship, and it immediately ap-
pealed to me as being serviceable because of the depth of
his ideas, and fascination because of the charm of his elo-
quence."[72] But like Augustine before him, whose understanding of friendship changed after his conversion, when
Aelred entered the monastery he noticed "the ideas I had
gathered from Cicero's treatise on friendship kept recurring
to my mind, and I was astonished that they no longer had
for me their wonted savor."[73] Aelred begins to ask what
friendship means for a Christian. He wants to know how
our understanding of friendship changes when it is seen to
exist not just between the friends, but as Augustine said,
with Christ as a partner.

There is no doubt for Aelred that friendship is a great
good, perhaps life's supreme good; certainly, like Aristotle

and Cicero, he cannot imagine life without friends. While discussing friendship with Walter and Gratian, two fellow monks, Aelred exclaims,

> I do not presume that I can explain it in a manner befitting the dignity of so signal a good, since in human affairs nothing more sacred is striven for, nothing more useful is sought after, nothing more difficult is discovered, nothing more sweet experienced, and nothing more profitable possessed. For friendship bears fruit in this life and in the next.[74]

Like Aristotle, Aelred speaks of three kinds of friendship, but only one is friendship truly because it alone can make us good as God wants us to be good. "Hence let one kind of friendship be called carnal, another worldly, and another spiritual," Aelred explains. "The carnal springs from mutual harmony in vice; the worldly is enkindled by the hope of gain; and the spiritual is cemented by similarity of life, morals, and pursuits among the just."[75] The similarity with Aristotle is striking. What Aristotle calls friendships of pleasure, usefulness, and virtue, Aelred calls friendships that are carnal, worldly, and spiritual. What distinguishes the friendships is whatever aim bonds the friends, for it is around that central desire the friendship, as well as the friends, will be shaped. Friendships are constituted by the good they are meant to achieve. Coming into contact with that good through the friend is the friendship's rationale and primary activity. Keeping this in mind, Aelred says the only friendship worthy of the name is one in which the friends are brought together in virtue of the God they both seek.[76] They are friends because each sees in the other the desire that is also her own, and they know the purpose of their friendship is not only to love one another, but in loving one another to love God as well. Their friendship embodies a hope, the hope that through the friendship they can touch God, the hope that their friendship will mediate to them the good they want to become.

Since every friendship takes the form of the good it seeks,

the foundation of spiritual friendship must be love of God.[77] When Aelred speaks of love of God as the basis for spiritual friendship, he means not only, like Augustine, that the friendship is a gift of God's love, but also that this love is the friendship's life, its vital principle, its abiding activity. Their friendship is the activity of God's love working freely between them. The vital principle of true friendship for Aelred is the friendship God is. Like Augustine, it is from this love that spiritual friendship is born, according to this love that it lives, and it is the fullness of this love it seeks.

The way Aelred commonly expresses how God must be the center of spiritual friendship is to speak of the friends living in and with Christ. When they are present to one another, Christ is present to them too. In Book I, when Aelred first sits down with Ivo, he says, "Here we are, you and I, and I hope a third, Christ, is in our midst."[78] As becomes clear when Aelred and Ivo talk—or as Aelred talks and Ivo listens—spiritual friendship seeks God by being in Christ. More than Augustine, Aelred forges a connection between the fullness of life in God, which is the goal of every friendship, and the ongoing life of the friends in Christ by which that fullness is attained. In this sense, spiritual friendship is christocentric, a paradigm of discipleship life. Kingdom life, friendship's goal, requires discipleship life with Christ. The friends seek God by living in Christ, the connection cannot be severed, for it is the history of their friendship in Christ that makes possible Kingdom life with God. After hearing Aelred's description of spiritual friendship, Ivo, as always, asks for more:

> I should like also to be instructed more fully as to how the friendship which ought to exist among us begins in Christ, is preserved according to the Spirit of Christ, and how its end and fruition are referred to Christ. For it is evident that Tullius was unacquainted with the virtue of true friendship, since he was completely unaware of its beginning and end, Christ.[79]

Aelred could not agree more. Cicero "was unacquainted with the virtue of true friendship" because he did not see that true friendships seek God. Like Augustine, Aelred understands friendships to be the way men and women return to God. We make our way back to God not as solitary travelers, but as fellow pilgrims, shoulder-to-shoulder en route to a Kingdom that has always been our home. But our return to God takes place in a special kind of relationship we have with one another. We journey to God through the friendship we have with one another in Christ. Spiritual friendship is our return to God. It is not just that as we seek God we happen to find ourselves alongside others; rather, we must seek God communally because God is found not apart from, not even at the end of, but always in and through the friendships of those whose life is one in Christ. "For what more sublime can be said of friendship," Aelred ponders, "what more true, what more profitable, than that it ought to, and is proved to, begin in Christ, continue in Christ, and be perfected in Christ?"[80]

What does Aelred mean by this? Christ is the principle of spiritual friendship—it is according to the life and example of Christ that the friendship must be measured. Spiritual friendship must achieve a Christlike life in the friends. When Aelred speaks of spiritual friendship beginning in Christ, continuing in Christ, and being perfected in Christ, what he is talking about is not simply union with Christ, but a way of life, a special kind of history. To be in Christ is to have our life take discipleship form. The friends can continue in Christ only when they fashion their lives according to Christ, becoming part of the gospel drama in which they try to master the Word by being conformed to the Word.

For Aelred, there is nothing accidental about eventual reunion with God. Union with God, that fullness of spiritual friendship, requires life in Christ, and life in Christ is life lived according to the gospel portrait we have of Jesus. By acquiring the ways of God revealed in Christ, by becoming adept disciples, the friends return to God. For Aelred

the Kingdom is the friendship relationship with God
achieved by discipleship friendship with Christ. Put differently, discipleship friendship with Christ is the history that
mediates Kingdom friendship with God. From Christ in
whom each friend loves the other, they mount to that Kingdom where all are "but one heart and one soul" in God.

> And so in friendship are joined honor and charm, truth and
> joy, sweetness and good-will, affection and action. And all
> these take their beginning from Christ, advance through
> Christ, and are perfected in Christ. Therefore, not too steep
> or unnatural does the ascent appear from Christ, as the inspira-
> tion of the love by which we love our friend, to Christ giving
> himself to us as our Friend for us to love, so that charm may
> follow upon charm, sweetness upon sweetness and affection
> upon affection. And thus, friend cleaving to friend in the spirit
> of Christ, is made with Christ but one heart and one soul, and
> so mounting aloft through degrees of love to friendship with
> Christ, he is made one spirit with him in one kiss.[81]

Like Augustine, Aelred sees these friendships bonded in
Christ as schools of love. In them we learn what form our
love for one another and God must take if we are to attain
the happiness of loving God and all others as God has
always loved us. Aelred says, "And, a thing even more
excellent than all these considerations, friendship is a stage
bordering upon that perfection which consists in the love
and knowledge of God, so that man from being a friend of
his fellow-man becomes the friend of God, according to the
words of the Savior in the Gospel: 'I will not now call you
servants, but my friends'."[82]

We are perfected in spiritual friendship because we not
only learn to love as God loves, but through that love we
are changed, we become godly. The perfection wrought by
charity marks the internal transformation of a person remade according to God. We said before that morality involves a way of life that changes us. It is a matter of conversion, of the ongoing refashioning of our life in the likeness

of the God who is our salvation. That perfection comes through spiritual friendship witnesses that every love brings likeness, and Christlike love brings likeness to God. It changes us so completely that God sees us differently, no longer as servant but as friend.

With the transformation of everyone from servant to friend, the Kingdom has come. For Aelred, the union of the friends in Christ prefigures the union of humanity in God. Aelred says, "Friendship, therefore, is that virtue by which spirits are bound by ties of love and sweetness, and out of many are made one."[83] Spiritual friendship works not only for a union among the friends, but for the union of all in God, and this union is possible only when everyone beholds one another not as stranger but as friend. If the witness of spiritual friendship is the unity of the Kingdom, the power of spiritual friendship is that through this love Kingdom unity is slowly brought to be. The power of any love is measured in the union it can achieve. For Aelred, the love at work in spiritual friendship is unsurpassable because it achieves not just a union in Christ between the friends, but goes beyond them to work for the union of all in God.

This is why their preferential love is Christian. Their preference for one another is also a preference for Christ and what Christ desires. It is not a narrowing of their world, but the explosion of their world, the explosion of all boundaries and restrictions, of all prejudice and elitism, of the selfishness that leaves so many unattended. With Christ they learn to love who God loves, they learn to love all their brothers and sisters, to go out to them not as strangers but as friends. In the love they have for one another, they see the Kingdom to which God's love tends, the Kingdom where each beholds the other as God does, in that Divine Friendship where the happiness of one is the happiness of all. Thus, their preferential love is inclusive, abiding as an invitation to others to experience the community through whom fullness of life comes. In a crescendo of joy, a song of praise and thanks to God, *Spiritual Friendship* culminates in this majestic vision of Kingdom unity, where "with salvation secured, we shall rejoice in the eternal possession of Supreme Goodness; and this friendship, to which here we admit but few, will be outpoured upon all and by all outpoured upon God, and God shall be all in all."[84]

God's Kingdom is a Kingdom of friendship, a Kingdom in which all have perfect unity with one another because all have perfect unity with God. It is not the end of spiritual friendship, it is its perfection; indeed, this Kingdom of friendship, humanity of one heart and mind with God, is the unity of all in Christ for which the friends always strove. Aelred describes this true and perfect friendship we call Kingdom:

> This is extraordinary and great happiness which we await, with God himself acting and diffusing, between himself and his creatures whom he has uplifted, among the very degrees and orders which he has distinguished, among the individual souls whom he has chosen, so much friendship and charity, that thus each loves another as he does himself; and that, by this means, just as each one rejoices in his own, so does he rejoice in the good fortune of another, and thus the happiness of each one individually is the happiness of all, and the universality of all happiness is the possession of each individual. There one finds no hiding of thoughts, no dissembling of affection. This is true and eternal friendship, which begins in this life and is perfected in the next, which here belongs to the few where few are good, but there belongs to all where all are good.[85]

Karl Barth

In many respects what Karl Barth says about Christian love bears pronounced similarity to Nygren's account of agape. Just as Nygren said agape had to be spontaneous, unmotivated, and indifferent to value, Barth says Christian love "does not turn to this other, the object of love, in the interests of the loving subject, either in the sense that it desires the object for itself . . . or in the sense that it attempts to perpetuate itself in its desire." No, "Christian love turns to the other purely for the sake of the other. It does not desire it for itself. It loves it simply because it is there as this other, with all its value or lack of value. It loves it freely."[86] Christian love is marked by self-giving, a movement in which one turns from himself to another "who is wholly different from the loving subject." It is an act in which the "loving subject reaches back . . . to give itself . . . to give itself away; to give up itself to the one to whom it turns for the sake of this object." In this act, Barth reflects, "the loving man has given up control of himself to place himself under the control of the other, the object of his love. He is free to do this. It is in this freedom that the one who loves as a Christian loves. Where this movement is fulfilled in all its aspects, and reaches its goal in this self-giving of the loving subject, there is Christian love."[87]

Barth contrasts Christian love, which originates in self-denial and expresses itself in pure self-giving, with "this other kind of love" that is essentially self-assertion. This second kind of love loves the other not simply because he or she is there and is due one's love, but because there is something in the other the lover wants, some quality or attribute the lover wants to possess and control—he loves not for the sake of the other, but because in loving the other he magnifies himself. "As the other promises something—itself in one of its properties—there is the desire to possess and control and enjoy it," Barth remarks. "Man wants it for himself: for the upholding, magnifying, deepening, broadening, illuminating or enriching of his own existence; or perhaps simply in a need to express himself; or perhaps even more simply in the desire to find satisfaction in all his unrest." This is selfish love, love that manipulates and exploits, love that sees the other as a means to one's gratifi-

cation and esteem. "And so it also takes place," Barth
concludes, "that the one who loves . . . merely asserts himself the more strongly in face of it as he wins and keeps and
enjoys it, since all the time it is himself that he has in view,
and his own affirmation and development that he seeks."[88]
Such a love is the "direct opposite of Christian love" because "in all its forms it will always be a grasping, taking,
possessive love—self-love—and in some way at some point
it will always betray itself as such."[89]

At this point, there is no indication that Christian love
absolutely excludes friendship, since this "other kind of
love" which is grasping, possessive, self-absorbed, and exploitative could hardly be called friendship. But Barth goes
further. The self-giving which constitutes Christian love
must be offered with no hope of return. The reciprocity
integral to friendship, Barth contends, cannot be an expectation of agape. In friendship the other is loved because one
spies in him a similarity of interests, values, and concerns
that one wants to share. But agape "requires identification
with his interests in utter independence of the question of
his attractiveness, of what he has to offer, of the reciprocity
of the relationship, or repayment in the form of a similar
self-giving. In agape-love a man gives himself to the other
with no expectation of a return, in a pure venture, even at
the risk of ingratitude, of his refusal to make a response of
love. . . . He loves the other because he is this other, his
brother."[90] Agape is "the self-giving of one to another
without interest, intention or goal; the spontaneous self-
giving of the one to the other just because the other is there
and confronts him."[91] In expecting no return, in seeking
no identity of interests or concerns, agape parts company
with friendship.

To this point, Barth does sound very much like Nygren.
He arrives at this description of how Christians ought to
love on the basis of how God has loved us. Just as Nygren
said agape originates in the fellowship we have with God,
Barth says agape is the Christian's response to what God

has revealed about God and ourselves in Christ. As Barth puts it, Christ is the Word by which God tells us we are loved. In Christ God draws to us in love, in Christ we receive the eternal reassurance that we are bound to God in love, a love we did not deserve. Our love for one another commemorates God's love for us. For Barth, God's agape enables our agape because we could never love one another so generously if we did not know ourselves so loved; we could never take the risk agape involves if we did not know how involved God has been with us.[92]

Christian love is a meditation on what it means to be loved by God. The more penetrating our awareness of God's love for us and the life that love gives us, the more likely the correspondence of our love to God's. "It never can or will begin of and with itself, or continue of itself," Barth says about Christian love. "In both its inception and progress it stands in absolute need of this basis. . . . That human love is dependent on divine love means that in its very freedom it can take place only on the basis of the latter, as a human response to the Word spoken in the love of God. . . . Man never can or will take the initiative in love. He can and will love only because God has first loved, and loves, him. . . . The love of God always takes precedence."[93]

Knowing God loves us, knowing what that love is and how absolutely we depend on it, the Christian loves in like manner not as a duty but as a desire, not because she is commanded but because she is grateful. The love of God "always has the character of grace, and that of man the character of gratitude."[94] God's love establishes fellowship and redeems; our love receives and says thanks.

Christian love is also a way of continuing God's love. For Barth, it is through the community of Christians that God's love breaks through. This does not mean God's love is mediated exclusively through the Christian community, nor that it is restricted to the community, but it does mean Christians live with the special awareness that they are to be God's people in the world, that they are entrusted guardians of God's love. As Barth sees it, "the love of God establishes fellowship between God and man," and on the basis of this fellowship, of what God has done for us and confided to us in Christ, we are "free to imitate His divine action in the sphere and within the limits of human action, and thus to love in human fashion as God does in divine."[95] Christians are called to love as God has loved them. For Barth, knowing the Word means living according to the Word. Knowledge of God's love in Christ always has practical implications; in fact, not to live according to the Word, not to practice it in our lives, indicates we have neither known nor understood the Word.

Barth says every Christian "is called to follow as a man the movement in which God Himself is engaged; to do as a man, and therefore in the form of a reflection or analogy, that which God does originally and properly."[96] Our love then is not only a continuation of God's love, but is the way we share in God's life. If we are "to follow as a man the movement in which God Himself is engaged," then in loving others as God has loved us, our love of neighbor is itself a participation in the life of God. In this way Barth, like Augustine and Aelred, recognizes that Christian love of neighbor is the way we move to God. By entering the life of our neighbor through love, we enter the life of God.

Barth contends that to love on the basis of what God has done for us in Christ entails being part of a people who make the same confession. Agape is community born from this confession of faith, it is itself a way of life. There will always be a special love alive between Christians, not because they are exclusive, but because they confess Jesus is Lord. "But—however irksome this may be to those who regard Christian love as a human virtue—it is still a closed circle: the circle of disciples, brothers, the saints, members of the body of Christ; the circle of the community of Jesus Christ gathered by the Holy Spirit from Jews and Gentiles, and ruled and quickened by Him," Barth writes, and even though "all men may . . . belong to this community," and even though "every man is called to enter it,"[97] still, "what the New Testament calls love takes place between Christians."[98]

Why is this? Because Christian love is more than a commemoration, it is a history. To pledge oneself to Christian love is to place oneself within a history of love, to become part of a drama of salvation which one's own love hopes to continue. Agape is the community of those who share this common memory and pledge to keep it alive, but it is also community formed from a historical event, the revelation of God in Jesus, that prompts a people to take up life a certain way. "That is to say," Barth elaborates, "as and because it is first a history between God and a people (Yahweh and Israel in the Old Testament and Jesus Christ and His community in the New) and only then a history between God and the world, between God and all men, the life of this people, the common life of its members, becomes part of the event and itself the history of salvation."[99]

Agape is a community's story that is part of the story of God. This is why Barth says, "Because these men are together in relation to God they are among one another in a very distinctive way. . . . It takes place unavoidably that there is a definite connexion of these men among themselves posited in and with their twofold passive and active relationship to God."[100] Agape is community, people joined to one another because of how God is joined to them. This does not make their love exclusive, but it does make it special. In a summary passage, Barth explains why loving God always engenders a community, why to have agape is always to stand with those who confess the same love.

> The one who loves God cannot then be solitary. He cannot be a religious individual with his individual concerns and joys and wishes and achievements. As one who has an active part in the history of salvation he is accompanied from the very outset not merely by fellows but by brothers, by those who

belong with him to the people of God, by fellow-partners in
the convenant, by the "household of faith" (Gal. 6:10). He
does not love God on the basis of a revelation directly vouch-
safed to him or in a private relationship. He began to love Him
as there was in the world—even before he himself was, or loved
God—the community which, called and gathered by the Holy
Spirit, attested the love of God to him, and summoned him
by its ministry to love God in return. And if he does love God
in return, this simply means that he for his part is called to
the same ministry and will live in and with the community.
But the life of the community, by whose ministry he is summoned to love God and in whose ministry he may participate
as one who does, is not the functioning of a mechanism but a
nexus of human relationships between those who have become
and are members of the one body, having their common Lord
and Head in the one person. To love God is, then, to live at
a specific point in this nexus, and at this point to be together
with the men who are also called to the service concerned and
participate in life in this service. To love God, since it is
always a question of definate action, is to stand at this point
in one of the many human relationships which exist here,
being united to this man or that by the fact that he too is
awakened by the love of God to love God in return. [101]

Though Barth never refers to the Christian community as a
community of friendship, the relationship he describes between those who confess Jesus is Lord is, in the terms of
our discussion, a friendship. Friendships arise between
those drawn together in agreement on what they consider
their life to be, and their friendship is the activity of pursuing this together. This is exactly how Barth describes the
Christian community. It is the fellowship of believers
joined together in the conviction that their life means nothing more than doing for others what God has done for
them—what "the members of the people of God have mutually to attest and guarantee is simply that God loves
them, and that they may love Him in return." [102] Barth

says each Christian is for the other a witness and confirmation "of that which is supremely important and indispensable,"[103] namely, that God's love is real.

Knowing this is no small reassurance. For Barth this is the knowledge one Christian gives to another. He can be certain of God's love for him because of the love his sisters and brothers show him. As Barth explains, the "truth and reality" of what takes place "vertically" between God and every person, must, if it is to be credible, be reflected in what takes place "horizontally" between one Christian and another.[104] In a passage of unusual poignancy and beauty, Barth wonders if without the love one Christian has for another, the love of God would ever be revealed.

> What, then, would I be, what would become of me, and how could I become and be and remain what I am as a member of God's people loved by Him and loving Him in return, if this being of mine, the being of the whole people of God as such and in it my being, were not continually proclaimed to me by the human action of the one who is a member with me, i.e., if he with his being did not guarantee the truth and reality of mine? What would I be if this other were not to me a witness of God, of the history of salvation in which my life too has a part, of the divine work which affects me too, of my liberation for the love of God? If this were the case, then on the level where man is confronted by man I should be referred to myself even in respect of the relationship between God and me and me and God, receiving neither light nor strength from my fellow. Would the love of God then be revealed? Would I be able to perceive it and respond to it? Without the ministry of the people of God and its members, would I be loved by God at all, or free to love Him in return?[105]

Agape describes friendships constituted by the desire to witness and sustain the love of God revealed in Christ. This love requires community because there is no other way for it to be real. Agape is a community of friendship because, as the Incarnation testifies, it cannot be without being historical, concrete, and embodied. The Christian community, in virtue of the friendship which abides among them, witnesses to a love that otherwise could not be known. Their friendship does not impede agape, it embodies agape; it brings agape to life. And so, even though Barth at one point says the reciprocity required for friendship makes it a love other than agape, his account of the Christian community as people joined to commemorate God's love for us in Christ makes agape the love of the friends of God. As Barth explains, it is this love they have for one another that makes tangible the love God has for all.

> But in the indirectness of this declaration the neighbour can and may and should and will guarantee to his neighbour, and the brother to his brother, the fact that God does really and truly love Him, and that he may really and truly love God. They and all the members of the people of God, each in relation to the other, need this declaration and are capable of it. And they are placed under this gracious law as mutual witnesses in order that they may by this means serve and help and uphold and comfort and admonish and therefore befriend one another—not as gods but as neighbours and brothers loved by God and loving Him in return.
>
> This witness will be genuine and useful to the extent that between man and man, with all the imperfection of what one man can be and do for another, there is a true reflection and imitation of what takes place between God and man, so that while there is no replacement of the latter, or identity with it, there is a similarity, and what is done is calculated to give a necessary reminder of it. [106]

Furthermore, though agape requires friendship, it is not restricted to friendship. The core of Barth's argument is that Christians love the world in and through the community of love they promise to be. Put more strongly, it is only insofar as they are a community of love that they can have agape for others. Agape requires this community, but agape is never confined to this community, nor does it exist for the sake of this community; agape exists for the sake of all those God loves. The circle of Christian love should always grow larger, extending itself from the community to others. In this way, their love lives not apart from the world, but as a way of transforming the world. It is precisely their preference for Christ that empowers their love for all. As Barth reminds us, "I love neither God nor my brothers if I do not show openly to every man without distinction the friendliness emphatically recommended and even commanded in so many New Testament passages."[107] Thus, Christian love ought to be an act of self-giving expressed to everyone, without calculation of the other's value or our possible return, but such an extraordinary love is possible only when it flows from a community whose love for one another is formed by and witnesses a God who is the Love by whom all things are.

In this chapter we have examined the charge of Kierkegaard and Nygren that friendship cannot be Christian love because preferential loves are at odds with universal love. While noting the strengths of their position, we suggested the claim only holds if the friendship in view is not Christian, that is, if the love between friends is something other than love for God. However, as our study of Augustine, Aelred, and Barth indicates, with love for God friendship not only does not oppose Christian love, but becomes the relationship in which that love is learned. Finally, given the internal connection between Christian friendship and Christian love, agape is not love beyond friendship, but Christian friendship's perfection.

In these first four chapters, we have spoken much of friendship with one another, but have said little about friendship with God, and that must be addressed. The Christian life, said St. Thomas Aquinas, is friendship with God. It is an exhilarating, if frightening, notion that we can be friends of God, but for Thomas this is what the Christian life is meant to be. Thomas called this friendship charity, and what he meant by it we shall consider next.

5. The Christian Life as Friendship with God:

What Aquinas Means by Charity

I. An Almost Blasphemous Claim: Why We Can Be Friends of God

When Thomas Aquinas writes so simply, so straightforwardly, in question 65, article 5, of the *Prima Secundae,* that "charity signifies not only love of God but also a certain friendship with God," a friendship "which consists in a certain familiar colloquy with God" which is "begun here in this life by grace, but will be perfected in the future life by glory,"[1] he uncovers the most mystical side of his vision of the moral life. Thomas believes the unimaginable; in fact, he insists on it. Thomas believes we can, are called to be, and must be friends of God. That is what our life is, a life of ever-deepening friendship with a God who is our happiness, a colloquy of love given and love received, a sharing in which each friend delights in the goodness of the other, seeks their good, desires their happiness, and finally becomes one with them.

But here the friend is God. What Aristotle found impossible, Thomas could confidently proclaim because of the Christian conviction that God's grace offers possibilities for happiness we could never achieve by ourselves. For Thomas, friendship is both the most accurate and the most hopeful way to describe what our life with God is and should be. Charity, this friendship with God, is the love with which the Christian life begins, the love by which it is sustained, and the love in which it is eternally perfected. But if it is the most promising love, it is also the most demanding love. Charity is the soul of the Christian paradox, for charity is the love which demands our self, but charity is also the love which promises a self. In friendship with God we give ourself away, we surrender to the Spirit, and in that surrender our most exquisite individuality is secured, for we come to be what God in perfect love has always wanted us to be.

It is an astonishing claim, an almost blasphemous claim, to think we can be, are called to be, and must be God's friends. Yet, such a spellbinding, unthinkable possibility represents for Aquinas what God wants every human life to achieve. For Aquinas it is our telos, the purpose to which every human being must aspire if they are to realize what being human means. When Charley Parker, Paradise golf pro of *Love in the Ruins,* stands before the mirror and says, "Charley, who in the hell are you? What does it all mean?"[2] Thomas has an answer. Charity, this friendship with God, is what it all means. To have charity is to have life, not to have charity is never to have had life, never to have known the God in whom our being resides. There is a single thing we are meant to do with our lives, a solitary purpose on which to make good, a purpose through which the meaning of everything else is known. We are called to achieve charity, to love in such a way that we become God's friends. Charity is a hauntingly beautiful possibility, and in this chapter we shall examine why this friendship can be ours and what this friendship means.

II. How Our Friendship with God Begins and Why It Is Happiness

As we saw with Aristotle, every friendship is based upon the good that bonds the friends and is shared between them;

the good that is communicated between them distinguishes the friendship. To understand the friendship that is charity and to know what makes this friendship different from others, we must consider the 'communicatio' from which it begins.[3] Thomas says it is God sharing with us God's very happiness. "Now there is a sharing of man with God by his sharing his happiness with us," he explains, "and it is on this that a friendship is based. . . . Now the love which is based on this sort of fellowship is charity. Accordingly it is clear that charity is a friendship of man with God."[4]

Aristotle said happiness is not a condition, but an activity, whatever activity which corresponds to a being's proper function. As we noted in chapter two, happiness is the best thing we can do, and for Aristotle it was the virtuous life. Thomas agrees with this, noting that each thing's happiness comes from what it does best, and then adding that in "God alone is it true that his very being is his being happy."[5] Whatever God is is God's happiness. God's happiness is not something extrinsic to God, but is something about the very life of God, God's utter actuality, the eternal activity that is God. God's happiness is whatever activity God essentially is; or, as Aristotle would put it, God's happiness is God's proper function. What is God's proper function, that special activity that distinguishes God?

Thomas says it is the friendship love between Father and Son that is Spirit. God's beatitude is God's actuality, and the perfect activity of God is the eternal friendship love between Father and Son, that exemplar generosity which begets Spirit. God's happiness, as Thomas sees it, is the friendship life that is God; it is this everlasting community of friendship love we call Trinity, where love offered is love wholly received and wholly returned, where the perfect mutuality of love between Father and Son is the Spirit of Love. For God to be happy is for God to be God, and for Thomas this means God being a Trinity of friendship between Father, Son, and Spirit. This friendship love that is the very life of God is what God does best. God's beatitude is the friendship love that is God, the perfect love relationship that is Trinity. Father, Son, and Spirit are one because that Spirit is friendship and that friendship, understood as God's life activity, is God's happiness.

What God 'communicates' to us when God offers us this happiness upon which our friendship with God is based is the friendship life who is God. Charity, Thomas says, is a friendship we have with God which begins in God's offer to us of the happiness who is God, and this happiness is God's Trinity of friendship. God, who desires to be friends with us, shares with us the friendship by which God is God, that friendship love between Father and Son, the nexus of which is Spirit, that is God's proper activity and, therefore, God's happiness. Our friendship with God begins when God diffuses in our hearts the happiness of God that is the friendship who is God. The gift from which charity begins is the outpouring of God's own happiness into our hearts, a divine happiness that is the divine friendship, a divine friendship that is the divine life.[6] Every friendship is identified by the good which joins the friends, which is the friendship's life, and the life of charity is this divine life, this sharing in, delighting in, and prospering in the beatitude of divine friendship. As Thomas says, it is a happiness we could never give ourselves; it is the gift, the unexcelled graciousness, upon which our friendship with God, and, therefore, our life, begins.

> Charity, as we have said, is our friendship for God arising from our sharing in eternal happiness, which is not a matter of natural goods but of gifts of grace, according to St. Paul, "The free gift of God is eternal life." Consequently charity is beyond the resources of nature, and therefore cannot be something natural, nor acquired by natural powers, since no effect transcends its cause. Hence we have it neither by nature, nor as acquired, but as infused by the Holy Spirit, who is the love of the Father and the Son; our participation in this love, as we said earlier on, is creaturely charity itself.[7]

What does Thomas mean by this? Left to ourselves there is no way we could have the happiness with God that is charity. When Thomas says no effect can transcend its cause, he reminds us that charity bespeaks a participation in the life of God that can only be a gift from God. The splendor of charity is its marvelous gratuity. Charity describes what must exist between God and ourselves if we are to exist, if we are to know what it is to be human, but what charity also describes is the absolute gift of God who offers us life we could never grasp ourselves.

To love God as friend is to love a God who always loves us first. It is God's movement toward us in love that allows us to move toward God in love. Thomas says we return to God in love only because God has come to us, in grace, in Word, in Spirit. Left to ourselves, hoping for this friendship is hoping too much. However, Thomas's point is that we are *not* left to ourselves, we are left to God, blessed with a possibility for happiness and wholeness only God can give. It is because of what God desires for us and because of what God desires to be for us that our desire for God can be met. Our hope is met by God's graciousness, which explains why our friendship love for God is always a kind of gratitude, a recognition that our need for God can be met only through God's love for us. We can seek through love the God upon whom our wholeness depends because this God has always dwelt in our hearts.

There is then a relationship between charity and grace. Charity is the fellowship we are called to have with God, a fellowship of which the Kingdom is perfection, but a fellowship which can only begin in grace. Charity is not itself grace, but it requires grace and grows from grace. In the language of the *Summa Contra Gentiles,* Thomas says grace is "the supernatural form and perfection" which is "superadded to men whereby they may be ordered suitably to the aforesaid end,"[8] and in the *Summa Theologiae* he describes it as a "kind of quality" infused in a person whereby he or she "may be moved by God sweetly and promptly towards obtaining the eternal good."[9] Grace is "a certain habitual gift, by which spoiled human nature is healed, and once healed, is raised up to perform works which merit eternal life."[10]

What Thomas recognizes is that if we are to have friendship with God, there must be a way that we are made to 'fit' this God. God is our happiness, but God is absolutely beyond us. In Thomas's language, we must be made 'proportionate' to God, we must fit the end we seek, and this is what grace achieves. Grace 'elevates' us to the end that is our fullness. Grace makes possible the kinship in which peace resides. It is the gift which enables the truly supernatural life we call charity because it brings the divine life into our hearts and makes the otherwise absolutely impossible the most genuine expression of who we are. With grace, the friendship with God that otherwise is hoping too much is the only true description of what being human means.

It is in this way that Thomas deals with the charge that God simply is too much unlike us for us ever to be God's friends. Aristotle said no matter how much we might want friendship with the gods, it never would be possible because friendship has to be between equals. Friendship requires the equality in which "each partner receives in all matters what he gives the other, in the same or in a similar form; that is what friends should be able to count on."[11] Elsewhere he speaks of the equality of friendship as an equality of goodness, a relationship in which the friends are equal in virtue.[12] In every example he offers, Aristotle implies too great a difference between people makes friendship impossible. If friendship has to be between equals, how can we have true friendship with God?[13]

Thomas knows we shall never have a friendship with God exactly like the friendships we have with others. We must speak analogously about our friendship with God; there must always be ways we qualify our description of this friendship, adjust our description to the uniqueness of charity. Thomas says charity is a "certain friendship" (*amicitia quaedam*) we have with God.[14] It is friendship of a sort, friendship of a special kind. But it is, for all that, still a friendship, and its possibility arises not in ourselves, but in the offer of God's grace which 'proportions' us to the God in friendship with whom we are perfected.

What grace enables charity completes. Because grace is the gift which both establishes and enables friendship with God, to live in charity is to live according to grace. Striking an analogy between nature and its operations, arguing that as a thing is so does it act, Aquinas says grace is the 'second' nature which makes the supernatural activity of charity possible. To act in charity is to act according to the grace in which we exist, the grace by which we are defined. If it is true that "as a thing is so does it act," then the supernatural activity of charity is entailed by what God's grace makes us. Viewed this way, charity is an implication of grace, an activity, a way of life derived from a genuine understanding of who we are. In grace we are not merely human, we are sharers in God's life, men and women who already participate in the friendship that is God; thus, to act in charity is to live in harmony with ourselves, to act according to, not in opposition to, who we truly are. When we make our life this friendship with God we help nurture and perfect, we help bring to completion, the sharing in God grace begins.

This is seen in Thomas's description of the friendship began by grace. He speaks of this friendship as *inchoatus*, a Latin word meaning something just beginning, something incomplete and unfinished. The life with God we have in grace is *inchoatus* inasmuch as it is a promise of glory that must be brought to fullness through charity's love. Grace grows through charity. Grace is the 'root' or 'germ' of charity, but charity is the fullness and completion of grace. The friendship with God that is our perfection is made possible through grace, but sustained through charity. What grace intends, charity achieves, this union of ourselves with God that is the harvest of a lifetime of friendship, of passionate seeking for God. In this sense, charity, and all the virtues born from charity, are nothing more than grace expressed in activity, for they accomplish day-by-day the transformation of our self unto God which grace enables and always intends. This is why Thomas says grace is a gift but charity is a virtue, the power or skill to make good on the promise of grace, to sustain and deepen the love that is our life. Grace is the love from which charity's love grows, sign that the gift which has been offered has also been received, making of our life an ongoing colloquy of love through which the promise of divine life is fashioned into the fullness of divine life, the perfect friendship that is Kingdom. In this way, all of us who are born God's children become God's friends. [15]

Furthermore, if what is infused in charity is the "love of the Father and the Son" we call Spirit, this friendship life of God, and if "our participation in this love . . . is creaturely charity itself," then growth in the Spirit is what charity's love intends. In fact, to be possessed by the Spirit is to have achieved fullness of friendship with God. The infusion of the Spirit begins our sharing in eternal happiness. Charity works to deepen our assimilation into this happiness.

To participate in the friendship of God is to be changed according to it, gradually to be remade according to the Spirit of Love. That is grace's goal and charity's work, that is the telos implanted in grace and achieved in charity, this transfiguration of ourselves in the Spirit. The perfection of our friendship in God is the fullness of God's friendship in us, the utter conformity of our lives to the Spirit, the union of ourselves in God's happiness.

When Thomas speaks of charity as our active participation in the Divine Friendship, he discloses what for him is the task and fullness of the Christian moral life. The purpose of the moral life is to make our way to God, to return to God through love. We return to God through love, but it is a union achieved not so much through our efforts to love, but through our surrender to Love, a union wrought from the Spirit freely at work in our lives. In grace God gives us the Spirit of Love, and it is through charity that we continue to share in it. The strategy of charity is to share so deeply in the Spirit of Love, to participate so fully of God's friendship, that ultimately we are one with it. The fullness of our life is foretold in the offer of grace. Our eternal happiness is sharing in God's eternal happiness. God's happiness is God's friendship life; thus, our happiness is a measure of the friendship life we have with God.

Finally, if our happiness is a measure of our participation in the friendship life of God, then we see that for Aquinas, as for Aristotle, happiness is not so much a state, but whatever activity brings about the fullest possible development of a human being. For Aquinas, this will be charity-friendship with God. As we saw in chapter two, Aristotle connected eudaimonia to a human being's most proper function. There is some activity or set of activities by which men and women bring themselves to the fullness for which they are created—Aristotle called this fullness eudaimonia, and the activities constitutive of eudaimonia the virtues. Thomas suggests the same. In question 3, article 2, of the *Prima Secundae,* Thomas asks if happiness is an activity. Not surprisingly, he answers yes. He says since "each thing is perfect inasmuch as it is actual, for what is potential is still imperfect," happiness "must go with man's culminating actuality. . . . That is why, in other things too, Aristotle says that each is for its activity. Therefore man's happiness has to be an activity."[16]

Happiness, what Thomas sometimes calls beatitude, describes a person who has reached the highest possible development proper to a human being. As for Aristotle, happiness belongs to the person who has achieved that for which human life is given, it inheres in the person who has reached her "culminating actuality," her highest potential being. Noting that Aristotle says that "each is for its activity," Thomas agrees that happiness is intrinsic to whatever activity, whatever special purpose or function, human life is given to achieve. It is not simply a condition of this fullness, but the activity which constitutes this fullness. Happiness really is the best thing we can do because through the activity proper to happiness we are brought to full development in our telos. As Thomas remarks, Aristotle hit the essence of happiness "by marking what puts man in this state, namely an activity of some sort; and he follows this line in the *Ethics* to show that happiness is the crowning good."[17] There is then an intrinsic connection between our happiness and the proper function or activity which mediates it. Happiness is lifelong involvement in the activity by which our grandest possibility is achieved.

For Thomas the telos of human life is union with God in friendship with God. We reach the fullness of our nature, the absolute perfection of ourselves, when we are united with God as friend through the love which makes that union possible. Our beatitude is perfect, everlasting friendship with God, and we achieve that through a life of charity. Our culminating actuality is Kingdom friendship, and it is through charity that this relationship with God is wrought.

And so just as Aristotle said that ultimately our telos, eudaimonia, and the virtues are one, so Thomas says charity and beatitude are one. Charity is not something different from our happiness, it is precisely the way of life that is happiness. Happiness is charity because friendship with God both constitutes and mediates the fullness for which we are made. Thus, beatitude is not something different from charity, but is the activity of charity perfectly realized. In short, friendship with God is our happiness because it is the comprehensive life activity by which we participate now, however partially, in Kingdom community.[18]

Thus far, we have shown how we can have friendship with God and why this friendship is our happiness. What we have not shown is what this friendship is. When Thomas says "charity signifies not only the love of God, but also a certain friendship with him,"[19] he has in mind a very special, distinct relationship between God and ourselves. Charity is not any love, it is friendship love. To be God's friend is more than to love God, it is loving God in a certain way, it is making our relationship with God conform to the elements determinative of friendship. A friendship is more than a relationship of closeness or general good feeling, it is a relationship defined by three characteristics which must be present. These are benevolence, or well-wishing, mutuality or reciprocity, and the capacity to look upon the friend as another self, a capacity derived from sharing in the good upon which the friendship is based. When Thomas says for us to love God we have to be God's friends, this is what he has in mind. We only truly love God when we have learned to be God's friend, and to be God's friend our relationship with God must be marked by the qualities integral to friendship. What those qualities are and what they mean is what we shall consider now.

III. The Three Marks of Friendship and What They Mean When the Friend Is God

All friendship is love, but not all love is friendship. What first distinguishes friendship love is that the focus of its love is the friend and the friend's well-being. As Thomas explains when he begins his study of charity, "According to Aristotle not all love has the character of friendship, but that only which goes with well-wishing, namely when we so love another as to will what is good for him. For if what we will is our own good, as when we love wine or a horse or the like, it is a love not of friendship but of desire."[20]

The first mark of friendship is benevolence. Benevolence is not only wishing our friends well, but actively working for their well-being, supporting their interests, seeking their good, and we do this because we love our friends not for the pleasure or usefulness we find in the friendship, we love them for their own sake. To "will what is good" for our friends is to want nothing more than what is best for them, and to see our participation in the friendship to be this active, genuine working for their good. We recognize that their good is our good, that precisely the joy of the friendship for us is our ability to do what is good for the friend we love.

Friendship reverses the direction of love's concern. Its love interest is not the pleasure or usefulness that accrues to one in being a friend of the other, but the happiness and well-being of the friend herself.[21] The strategy of friendship is to discover one's own good not by directly seeking it, but by devoting oneself to the good of the other. In this way, one's own good is the friend's good, one's own happiness is seeking the happiness of the friend. The project of any good friendship is to discover that working for their good is our happiness not only because we love them, but because the good we seek for them is also the good we want for ourselves. Because they love what we do, there is nothing we want more than to offer them the good they bring to us.

Thomas says all love "consists in wanting good things for someone. . . . The movement of love therefore has a two-fold object: the good thing which is wanted for someone, whether oneself or another person, and the one for whom it is wanted. The former is the object of love-of-desire; the latter is the object of love-of-friendship."[22] All love shares in common a desire for a particular good, but what distinguishes loves is the one for whom the good is desired and the reason it is desired. Friendship is the love whose whole thrust, whose total energy, toils for the good of the other, not because the one who loves has no good of his own, but because what he loves and sees as his good is the good of his friend. Benevolence implies not only that the friend is loved for herself, but also, because she is loved, the active seeking of her good is the sustaining project of the lover's life. This is what friendship is, mutual devotion to the good of the other because it is a good both share. Friendship is the activity where each works for the other's well-being, the activity in which each is dedicated to prospering the other's good. Nothing is more delightful, nothing more life-giving for the friend, because the good for which they work is the good which makes them friends. Applied to charity, benevolence means we seek God's good for God's sake, we endeavor to make God's will our own. Friends of God are those whose whole life project is to will what God wills as God wills it, to make God's good their own. Thus, charity is a life given to seeking and promoting what God wants, and seeing this as the singlemost meaning of one's life.[23]

And yet, there must be something more to friendship than benevolence. The devotion benevolence entails, if it is not returned, can be both frustrating and destructive. There is nothing sadder or lonelier than to be devoted to someone who shows no affection for us. This is why Aquinas says the benevolence of friendship must be mutual. Benevolence is necessary for friendship, but not sufficient. To be friendship, the well-wishing one offers another must be returned to the other in kind. This is the second mark of friendship. Friendship is a mutual or reciprocal love, a love in which each person knows the well-wishing she offers the other is returned to her. As Aquinas explains when he delineates the qualities of friendship, "Yet good will alone is not enough for friendship for this requires a mutual loving; it is only with a friend that a friend is friendly. But such reciprocal good will is based on something in common."[24]

Friendships cannot be one-sided. We may love another dearly, we may devote ourself to seeking her good, we may will nothing except what makes her happy, but even though that might be a splendid love, if it were not reciprocated, it would not be a friendship. Friendships are relationships in which each person knows the good he wishes for the other is also the good the other wishes for him. As Thomas noted, the reciprocity necessary for friendship is based on the good intrinsic to the friendship itself. What each friend seeks for the other is this shared good, this good both want for themselves. Friendship has to be reciprocal for the life of the friendship, this ongoing participation in the friendship's good, to be possible. Unless what we work for in the other is returned by them to us, the project by which friendships are known cannot occur.

We sense the importance of reciprocity for friendship when we consider those times when the love we offered was never returned. There remains an incompleteness to any love that is not met by love. Friendships live when love meets love, where one gift of love embraces another. Friends are those who recognize each other's love, exchange it, and whose sharing in that love keeps the friendship alive. As Robert Johann remarks,

> For friendship, it is not sufficient to love another directly as myself; to be friendship, my love of benevolence must be explicitly reciprocated. Friendship exists only between those who love one another. Thus it is conceived as adding to a one-sided love of benevolence a certain society of lover and beloved in their love.[25]

Johann's description of friendship as a "certain society," a miniature community of sorts, is telling, for it illustrates how friendship is the ongoing relationship we have with people we love in which goods and values are exchanged. Friendships are not something we turn on and off nor relationships we step into and out of; rather, friendships constitute our lives, they comprise the basic description of ourselves. We not only locate ourself in our friendships, our self is derived from our friendships. Every friendship constitutes a way of life, a special way of being a self. We are what the "society" or "community" of friendships makes us. To find a friend is to find a particular way of being a self. Friendships are the societies established and sustained by those who mutually enrich one another because they nurture one another from the goods both want to embody.[26]

This is the logic behind Aristotle's remark that friends who never spend time together do not stay friends for long. If friendship is the society of those who share the same good and through their friendship offer it to another, then friendship must be a life together. Aristotle argued that "those who extend friendship to one another without living together are more like men of good will than like friends. For nothing characterizes friends as much as living in each other's company."[27] Friends have to spend time together, they have to live in each other's company because that is what a friendship is. Aristotle knew that "the most desirable thing" for friends "is to live together" because "whatever his existence means to each partner individually or whatever is the purpose that makes his life desirable, he wishes to pursue it together with his friends."[28]

But he not only "wishes to pursue it together with his friends," he *has* to pursue it together with his friends because there is no other way for him to achieve his good than through the society of friends who share it. Friendship is this society among those who agree on the good they seek, and as a society, a partnership in the good, it is the life activity constitutive of oneself. We need to be with our friends not just because we wish to share this good with them, but more crucially because it is through them that we are endowed with our good. Friendship is the constitutive moral activity of our life because through it we receive from another the good with which we have identified ourselves. Friendship's rationale is to be the community in which the formation of the friends in the good they seek takes place. And that good in which we see ourselves completed is not something we can offer ourselves, it is only something we can receive from a friend whose love continually offers it. Selfhood is a matter of appropriating goods which enable fullness; in Thomas's language, it is a matter of appropriating God. But it is our friends who put us in touch with our good, who mediate to us the good by which we are. We reach what we desire through our friends, they are the ones whose love forms us in what we hope to become.

If our life is the friendships we have with those whose love completes us, then this is especially true of the society of friendship we have with God. In his *Scriptum Super Sententiis Magistri Petri Lombardi,* Thomas speaks of friendship as a certain society of lover and beloved in love, and then refers specifically to charity as a friendship we have with God in which God loves us and we love God, this mutual exchange of love effecting a society or partnership between God and ourselves.[29] If every friendship is the society we have with others based upon goods friends share, charity is the society we have with God based upon the happiness of God from which the friendship begins. The good of charity is the outpouring of the Spirit in our hearts. The strategy of our friendship with God is to foster the full assimilation of ourselves in the love from which charity begins. Like every friendship, charity has a task, to be the life activity through which we embody the good God offers us, the good without which we cannot be a self. If we are when we are what God wants us to be, someone transfigured in the Spirit of love, then we become this in friendship with the God who offers it.

Life in this Spirit is the fulsome good with which we have identified ourselves, the good in which we see ourselves completed, but it is not a good we can offer ourselves, it is only a good God can offer. This gift offered and received is charity's activity, charity's life. Every friendship thrives on the gift that is exchanged. Charity thrives on the offering and reception of God's life, God's happiness. And just as we said the indispensable value of any friendship is that it is our friends who put us in touch with our good, it is in charity that God puts us in touch with the Spirit. Charity mediates fullness of life because in the crucible of charity we both receive and conform to the Spirit of love. Like Aristotle's friends, we want to live in company with God; it is the most desirable thing for us, because what constitutes God's life, this Spirit of love, is the gift which also constitutes our own. It is our most splendid moral activity because it offers our most promising self. In charity, God puts us in touch with God.

This may be why Thomas also speaks of friendship as a "conversation" in the good. The "con-vivere" or life together of the friends is a "conversation" in the good which joins them. It is appropriate to speak of the society of friendship as a conversation in the good because it reminds us that the focus of friendship is not primarily the friends, but the good which joins them. To be friends they must be turned to the good they love, and they must understand their friendship to be a conversing in this good, an ever deepening participation in the good. This conversation in the good of the friendship makes possible the conversion to the good the friendship intends.

When Thomas speaks of friendship this way he has charity in mind. The friendship we have with God must be understood as a "conversation" with God in the good of charity.[30] But as the word suggests, to converse in the good of charity is to be changed by it. Charity is a way of being a self, but more exactly of becoming a self, of being transformed by the good of charity, of being transfigured in the Spirit. If the project of the moral life is to become more than we already are, then charity says it is to become godly, but specifically to embody the Spirit who is God's first and lasting gift to us. The conversation in the Spirit that is charity is the conversion to the Spirit who is love, and this conversion is understood to be the thorough remaking of ourselves unto God.

The project of the moral life is to become a certain kind of person. The project of charity is to be imbued with the Spirit, to be turned inside out by a love in which we lose one kind of self and take on another. If we are happy to the degree that we become godly, then charity is beatitude because it is the lifelong conversion of ourselves to the goodness of God. In every friendship we take on the form of the good the friends love. In charity we take on the form of God, we are formed in the Spirit, qualified by God's friendship love, that is how we are remade and that is why charity is our happiness, the most fulsome development of ourselves. Charity develops us because through this lifelong turning of ourselves to God we become who we were not— we become godly, we become holy people, we become people in whom God shines. Every love changes us, but only charity changes us unto God. Exactly our hope is that we cannot love God and remain the same. No one who is a friend of God remains the same, and that is the tremendously reassuring sign that we do not hope for goodness in vain. In charity we become exactly who we need to become, we begin to hint of holiness.[31]

In Book Three of his *Summa Contra Gentiles,* Thomas says "the ultimate end of things is to become like God," and this happens insofar as "created things . . . attain to divine goodness."[32] This is the strategy of charity, to bring us a likeness to God deep enough, a resemblance to God strong enough, that we are able to know and enjoy the happiness God enjoys. Every love brings likeness, and charity brings a likeness to God which enables us to be a friend to God. To be someone's friend, Aquinas knows, is to be "another self" to them, to be so alike not just in tastes and interests, but in character, in goodness and virtue, that they come to look upon us as a reflection of themselves.[33] The third mark of friendship is that through the love that bonds the friends, the love in which their friendship is a participation, each becomes for the other another self. This is akin to Aristotle's idea that the friend is like a mirror for us. We can see ourselves in them because we know we too have been formed, shaped, defined by the same love. They are like ourselves because through the friendship they have come to embody the same good.

The same is true when our friend is God. We cannot love God and remain unchanged. To love God in charity is to become like God in goodness. There is a terrible vulnerability in any love because to love is to become like the one we love. There is a loss of control in this, indeed a loss of self, because to love is to lose one kind of self and take on another. Nowhere is this transformation more drastic than in charity. Charity fosters vulnerability to God, an openness so exhaustive that we ultimately become defenseless before the love that is our life. To become defenseless before God in charity is fully to absorb the Spirit, to be made over by the love that is God's happiness. When that transfiguration is effected we have not only changed, we have changed in a way that makes us enough like God to be another self to God; it is then we can truly speak of ourselves as God's friends. The purpose of the moral life is for us to become for God who God has always been for us, a friend who seeks our good and wishes our perfect happiness—this is the possibility charity offers. When we can behold God as God always beheld us, as another self, a friend whose happiness is perfectly our own, a friend whose will is always what we seek, then beatitude has been gained; a lifetime of charity has made us enough like God to have union with God.[34]

Both H. D. Simonin and Richard Egenter explain this third mark of friendship by saying it describes a "similitude of being" wrought from friendship love. Simonin, for instance, speaks of the resemblance between God and ourselves effected by charity as an "ontological similitude,"[35] and Egenter suggests this "similitude of being is both the effective cause and sustaining principle of friendship."[36] Both are groping to express Thomas's claim that through charity's love we become another self to God. It is important that Simonin and Egenter speak of this not as an identity of being, but as a similitude of being.[37] To become another self to God does not mean we become God, nor that there is no longer any difference between God and ourselves. Love brings likeness, not identity. In making us another self to God, charity does not abolish differences between God and ourselves, it works for the union of hearts that is every friendship's perfection. The most perfect and lasting union requires a likeness based on goodness and love. If our perfect happiness consists in our perfect union with God, then this is nothing other than the relationship we have with God when we are another self to God. It does not mean we are lost in God, that God's love overwhelms our own; nor does it mean we are annihilated in God, as if God's love destroys our self. No, God's love does not destroy our self, it brings our self to its ultimate perfection, a self so imbued with God's goodness that we can consider ourselves not God, but another self to God.

There is a problem in this idea of becoming another self to God if we interpret it to mean there is no longer any difference between God and ourselves. Charity makes us like God, but it does not make us God. If charity is truly friendship, it makes us more fully someone who is not God, it makes us more fully ourselves. We can only have a friendship with someone who is not ourselves. If charity made us identical to God, then our friendship with God would be over for we would no longer be the 'other' every friendship requires. To say that in charity we become another self to God means the more we become like God, the more we become someone other than God, namely, ourselves. In becoming godly, in being formed in the goodness of God, we become our most genuine selves. It is exactly this perfection of otherness, an otherness rooted in divine goodness, which enables the most splendid flourishing of friendship with God. What friendship achieves is not an identity of selves, but the most genuine differentiation fostered by a love for the most genuine good, and that is why the likeness to God charity brings is really the most radical individuation. We can consider God another self because in charity God's good is our good; however, it is in making God's good our own that we most fully become not God, but ourselves.

What happens in any friendship is that in some ways the friends become more alike, in some ways they become increasingly different. As friendships grow, likeness increases inasmuch as the interests, concerns, values, and ideals of the friends become similar. On the other hand, difference increases too, because the deeper and longer our friendships with others, the more we become ourselves. The same is true in our friendship with God. We become more like God because we come to love what God loves, we make God's good our own; but we also become more unlike God because we become more genuinely ourselves. From loving God we grow into ourselves, that is what charity teaches us. To the degree we become like God in goodness, we become someone other than God. To the degree we become someone other than God, we can have the perfect happiness that is perfect friendship with God. With charity, both the likeness and the difference are rooted in the good from which the friendship begins.

Finally, although to speak of God as another self does not mean God's self becomes our own, it does mean we cannot be ourself without God. When we tell a friend she is another self, we imply it is hard for us to imagine ourself without her. If that is true in every good friendship, it is eminently true in friendship with God. To call God another self is a confession of need, a frank awareness that we need God in order to be. To speak of God as another self does not say charity makes us identical to God, but it does acknowledge that we have a self insofar as we share the life of God. To speak of God as another self is a reminder that what it means for us to be a self is to be God's friend, a reminder that God is the one by whom we always are. God is another self to us because our self is our friendship with God. What it means for any of us to be is to be God's friend, and that is why our fullest self is acquired when we are able to look upon God as another self.[38]

What kind of love puts no limit on the happiness God wants us to enjoy? This is the question which guides Thomas's understanding of the relationship which must exist between God and ourselves, and this chapter has tried to explain Thomas's answer. Our relationship with God is meant to be a friendship with God because friendship achieves a likeness to God which enables us fully to find happiness in God. Our happiness is a measure of our likeness to God, and there is no greater likeness than that which charity brings. God's hope for us is for us to enjoy the happiness that is God, the lovelife of God, God's Trinity of Friendship. God's plan is for us to share in the life of God, in a sense, to be able to enjoy God as God enjoys God. If it sounds incredible, perhaps even preposterous, that is only a measure of our hope and God's love. For Thomas, the fantastic is the true: we really can be friends of God. For Thomas, to be Christian is to live in friendship with God and to consider this extraordinary possibility the ordinary way of understanding our lives. The plot of Thomas's moral theology is to help us see that to be is to be God's friend. The grand and boundless possibility of every life is the union with God charity promises. It is a union based on likeness, an intimacy secured through the transformation of ourselves unto God. If the deepdown desire of our hearts is to find that peace in which we desire no more, then charity is a way of life which can match that desire. Thomas realized this, and it explains why his moral theology is the impassioned plea of a man who wants us to love God as deeply and thoroughly as we possibly can, who wants us to love God as friend. No other love will satisfy us because no other love brings us so deeply into God. This is what charity teaches, this is the intimacy charity achieves. It is one love that does not deceive.

6. Friendship and Everyday Life:

Discovering the Source of our Moral Deliverance

I. Taking a Chance with Others: The Beginning of the Moral Life

We cannot be moral until we learn to appreciate what is not ourself. That has been the chorus rumbling in the background of this book. It is time to bring it forward. We began our reflections by speaking of the need for a different model of the moral life. We were dissatisfied with many current approaches to ethics, not only because of their heavy emphasis on problems and decisions, but because they tended to be so individualistic, isolating a person from her or his relationships to others as well as failing to see why those relationships were morally important. The argument of this book is straightforward: The moral life is what happens to us in relationship with others. That appears a simple claim, but it has complex implications. It argues strongly for a relational approach to ethics. It insists that relationships are not external to the self but constitutive of the self. It suggests we stand not apart from or over against others, but in deep connection with them and all of life, a connection we rarely perceive and only dimly appreciate. That our relationships constitute our self is why friendships have such grand moral importance, whether that friendship be with God or a soulmate of many years.

So far we have discussed how these friendships school us in the good. We have suggested why they are not at odds with Christian love but really the relationships in which Christian love is learned. And we have considered what friendship means when the friend in mind is God. But we need to bring these reflections down to earth. We need to root them in the everyday. If the moral life happens through friendship, what exactly is it that happens to us? If we *are* through the relationships we have, especially our friendships, then what do these friendships do to us? Put differently, what does it mean to say the moral life begins for us when we learn to appreciate what is not ourself? To answer these questions and to show what it means to live the moral life as friendship is the purpose of this final chapter. It may be best to begin with a story.

At the beginning of my introductory course in ethics, I tell the students I am going to share with them my most memorable, formative moral experience. It is not what they expect. Most presume it will be a problem, for so often we conclude problems are what ethics is about. Others think for a moment and say it has to be some momentous decision, but I do not remember making any great decisions, usually I just fall into them and call them decisions retrospectively when I am trying to make some sense of my life.

No, to the dismay of the students I confess that my most memorable, formative moral experience came in the summer of 1976, when I was working in a chaplaincy program at Methodist Hospital in Brooklyn. But it did not happen at the hospital, it happened on the F Train, the subway which runs between Brooklyn and Manhattan. Every Friday after work I would board the F Train and ride into Manhattan for the weekend. At the height of the Friday afternoon rush hour, crushed in between bodies of all shapes and sizes, there were times the experience seemed more immoral than not, but that, I discovered, was a matter of perspective.

I had been riding this train every weekend, not paying

much attention to what was going on around me, but then, one Friday, I began to look. I looked at everyone in the car, I wondered about them—who they might be, where they might be going, what their lives might be like, what problems and struggles they might have, whom they might love and who might love them. The more I wondered about them in their private worlds the less private mine became. I looked around the car at all those people, people of different nationalities and backgrounds, people of richly different talents and gifts, people of complex, intriguing personalities, and suddenly, amidst all that diversity, I felt one with them. It was an awakening, one of those moments which turns our life around, an experience which makes us see the world differently. We all have had those moments, experiences so riveting that henceforth nothing is ever quite the same. They are experiences of insight, experiences which change us, and maybe they are experiences of conversion because after them we look at life with freshly baptized eyes.

Rocking back and forth on the train that afternoon, I looked at all those people, people whose otherness was startling, and felt a novel kinship with them. We were all very different, yet we were one; we comprised many worlds, yet together we made one world. I felt a peculiar intimacy with those people, a togetherness, even an indebtedness, for I began to see how much we need one another, how much we depend on the kindness of people we really do not know. It was a strange and liberating feeling, this mysterious mingling of differences and unity, and for me, oddly enough, it marked the start of the moral life, the birth of a different way of seeing the world.

On the F Train that afternoon, I realized how good it is to be together with strangers, how much we really want to love them even if we never come to know them, because to love them is to realize we cannot be ourselves without them. That is what genuine moral experience is, learning to appreciate what is not ourselves, and it is why friendship is such a fitting model for the moral life. Learning to appreciate another, coming to see how different they are from ourselves yet how much we depend on them, is just what friendship requires and what friendship teaches. We learn that all morality begins in and is an elaboration of the discovery that something other than ourselves is real—whether it is nature, another person, or God—and the moral life is the ongoing attempt to understand, deepen, and apply that discovery. Morality is an implication of otherness, and this means we can only be moral when we learn to appreciate what is not ourselves.

That is the most difficult and unsettling moral discovery we can make. Despite how obvious it is that something other than ourselves is real, it is something we stubbornly resist seeing because to acknowledge the other means we must acknowledge other points of view, other ways of understanding and valuing. To acknowledge worlds other than our own is to expose some of our own biases and misperceptions, to discover that so many of our cherished opinions may be wrong, so many honored practices unjust. This is unsettling. It involves what Thomas W. Ogletree calls a "decentering" of self, because it collapses our world and challenges our once unassailable sense of sovereignty. "The import of the other's expression in discourse is that it calls into question my egoism, which includes the sovereignty of my own meaning-constituting activity toward the world," Ogletree writes. "It confronts me with an appeal to take into account another center of meaning in my own understanding of the world, a center which in the nature of the case cannot be assimilated into my own processes of self-integration."[1]

Acknowledging the other makes us look differently at our world, and if this is true in chance encounters, it is eminently true in friendship. Friendship repositions us by drawing us out of ourselves, by pulling us beyond the confines of our own narrow world into the sometimes vastly different world of the other. There is always an uprooting, a sense of displacement, in the beginning stages of a friendship. There is often death to one way of thinking and birth to some things we had not considered before. To acknowledge another is to make our world bigger, to open it to surprise. It is impossible to risk such hospitality without feeling a loss of self, without an initial sense of disintegration, for that is exactly what happens. In acknowledging the other we travel into another's way of life and encounter there perspectives and hopes, fears and possibilities, which not only question so much we had taken for granted before, but invite us to consider the world anew. All this happens when we risk being someone's friend. As Ogletree explains, morality takes a different shape when it begins not with our own point of view, but when we suffer the hospitality that allows the stranger to become a friend.

> To offer hospitality to a stranger is to welcome something new, unfamiliar, and unknown into our life-world. . . . Hospitality designates occasions of potential discovery which can open up our narrow, provincial worlds. Strangers have stories to tell which we have never heard before, stories which can redirect our seeing and stimulate our imaginations. The stories invite us to view the world from a novel perspective. They display the finitude and relativity of our own orientation to meaning. The sharing of stories may prove threatening, but not necessarily so. It may generate a festive mood, a joy in celebrating the meeting of minds across social and cultural differences. The stranger does not simply challenge or subvert our assumed world of meaning; she may enrich, even transform, that world.[2]

Morality begins in this acknowledgment of the other that is the threshold of every friendship. Following the thought of Immanuel Levinas, Ogletree says the decentering involved in this experience is "not a threat to personal integrity, but . . . a summons to moral existence. Morality begins precisely when my egoism has been called into question and I learn to take the other into account. And egoism in this context," he explains, "refers not to selfishness in a crass sense, but to any process, however refined, in which I remain the decisive and controlling reference point for the meaning and value of the world."[3] Our moral adventure commences when we allow our encounter with another to draw us out of ourself. It is the adventure of another person shaping, challenging, and enlarging our world as we do their own. This may sound disconcerting, but it is not rare; indeed, it is part of the history of every friendship.

The plot of the moral life is to move beyond the security but hopelessness of egotism to the risk but enrichment of hospitality, and this is one thing friendship achieves. To be moral is to take a chance with another, to abide the kind of vulnerability which not only allows us to be changed by another, but suffers the stranger to become our friend. It is a risky, frightening, sometimes disappointing affair, this hospitality to strangers, but without it, Ogletree confides, morality "is but the shrewd management of life's exigencies in light of my more or less arbitrary personal preferences. Whether it be refined and subtle and sophisticated, or careless and thoughtless and unreflective, such morality finally boils down to egoism, the assessment and utilization of all aspects of the world in terms of my own purposes."[4] One reason friendship is such a fitting model for the moral life is that in friendships precisely the encounter with another necessary to free us from self-absorption occurs.

Never to acknowledge that something other than ourself is real is a kind of moral suicide. If morality begins in the acknowledgment of another and the invitation to seek communion with worlds other than our own, then not to respond, to choose to remain wholly within ourself, is to separate ourself from the others upon whom our deliverance depends. What we learn in the moral odyssey is that our moral deliverance, our wholeness and completion, ultimately come not from ourself, but from those others we allow to become part of our life. The greatest moral challenge is also the most essential. We have to learn to acknowledge the other because they are the key to our moral wholeness. This is what friendship attests. Our moral deliverance lies not in our hands, but in the hands of another, ultimately, to be sure, in the hands of God. And what sometimes makes this so disenchanting is that the ones who can do the most for us are precisely the ones most different from ourself, the ones who come into our world with a goodness we may even fear.

Riding the F Train on a Friday afternoon is a humbling, poignant moral experience because it reminds us how much we are changed and enriched when we suffer the kindness of those unlike us, when we receive the world of another as gift, an invitation to enlarge our life by entering, even if only momentarily, their own. As Blanche DuBois said at the end of Tennessee Williams's play, *A Streetcar Named Desire,* "Whoever you are—I have always depended on the kindness of strangers."[5] Those are words all of us can make our own. At some point all of us have been blessed, rescued, and redeemed by strangers we have chanced to see as friends. We have all had our hour of need when we were visited with a kindness, a smile, a word of encouragement from someone whose name we never learned, whose face we never saw again, but whose memory abides as testimony of how so much of who we are is the work of strangers we have chanced to see as friends. What is remarkable about the moral life is not that morality is friendship, but that all our friends were once our strangers. What is remarkable about friends is what a risk it is to let a stranger become one. But we take that risk. No matter how many times we might be hurt, even betrayed, by those to whom we risked ourselves, we continue to take a chance with them because intuitively we know we cannot abide a self without them. That morality takes the form of friendship is an implication of the others without whom we cannot be.

II. The Shape of Our Encounter with Another

One of the most insightful studies of how morality begins in an encounter with another is Enda McDonagh's little book, *Gift and Call*. McDonagh begins by isolating our basic moral experience. He wants to pinpoint the core of every moral experience, some single element present in all the experiences to which we rightly give the name "moral." If we took all these experiences and broke them down to their most common element, what would it be? What is the cornerstone of every genuine moral experience?

McDonagh says our primary moral experience is what happens to us when we stand in the presence of another.[6] The experience is moral because the sheer presence of the other person demands our attention. We experience their presence as a call to come out of ourselves. The other person impinges on us, their presence compels us to acknowledge that the experience is no longer one of solitude, but of otherness. The experience is moral because we sense we cannot be indifferent to their presence without misunderstanding the experience itself. As McDonagh sees it, the experience takes the form of a call, a summons to respond, and not to do so is to violate the meaning of the moment.[7] There is something unconditional and absolute about the call. We can respond in various ways, and there are obviously degrees to the kind of response that is demanded, but there is nothing optional about the call to respond. "The specific character of the call as distinct from its content is a certain unconditionality or absoluteness," McDonagh says. "Again the exact word to be used is hard to find. What I am trying to express is the way in which the moral call impinges on one as a call to which one ought to respond."[8]

We cannot choose not to respond and still claim to be moral. The basic moral duty of our lives is to recognize and respond to those who come our way. To refuse to respond is to betray the meaning of our most basic moral experience, it is to signal that at its most basic level we do not understand what morality involves, or if we do understand, we choose not to be involved in it. For McDonagh, to refuse to respond to another is to choose not to have a moral life. If morality originates in this call coming forth from another, to fail to heed the call is to decide to be immoral.

Furthermore, while the person who stands before us cannot be dismissed, neither can their otherness. To acknowledge them is to abide their otherness; it is to see they are not who we are, but clearly and intriguingly other. We betray the experience if we respond to them by attempting to make them like ourselves. We pervert the experience if our response becomes a manipulation, a kind of imperialism in which we will receive them into our life only on the condition that they serve our plans, that they become instruments to our purposes. In order to be moral, we must let their otherness be.[9] It is their definitive, irreducible otherness which constitutes the moral situation, and this means we cannot be moral by trying to deny or reduce their otherness; no, we can only be moral when we realize it is precisely their being part of a world other than our own that allows them to be a blessing for us.

An example of this is parents' relationship to their children. Parents have hopes for their children and values or ideals that guide how they raise their children; yet, it does not take any parent long to realize the 'otherness' of their children, to sense their unique personalities, their distinctive gifts, all those things which continually make children a surprise in their lives. Every parent knows to love their children they must let their otherness be. The only way children truly can be gifts to their parents is when the parents remember the ones their love brought into the world are other than themselves.

The same is true in all our relationships, person to person, community to community, nation to nation. To respect another we must let their otherness be. Morality involves not just a response to another, but a response formed from respect. A moral response is not one which tries to make another like ourselves, but one which realizes despite all the similarities which may exist between us, what we are ultimately called to respect and share is their otherness.[10]

What does this tell us about the shape of a moral response? If morality originates in this encounter with another whose presence demands recognition, and whose presence is experienced as a call to come out of ourself in response, then, McDonagh reasons, all genuine moral response is "other-directed" or "other-centered." There is a specific direction to moral behavior, a movement away from ourself to another. The explicit dynamic of morality is to become part of a world larger than our own through love. This is possible when we respond in trust and affirmation to all the others who come our way. Morality works for the liberation of ourselves, but such liberation can only come from others, and ultimately from God. We are freed from the prison of self-centeredness, from the wearying stratagems of egoism and fear, when we accept the invitation of another to become part of their world. In a way, this was Thomas's understanding of charity. The project of charity was to move us from self-absorption to God-absorption. In charity we respond to God's offer of love, God's invitation to come out of the unpromising confinement of our own world in order to find eternal life in God's. To have become God's friend through charity was to have recognized and responded to the otherness of God, to have spied that otherness not as something which would destroy us, but as the only love in which we ultimately could find life. Thomas's sense of charity parallels McDonagh's sense of the call embodied in the other. In their otherness they are the key to our liberation because it is only in becoming part of worlds larger than our own that we understand what it means for us to be a self.

The structure of moral experience then is away from self to another. It is this ongoing challenge to move from isolation to communion through love, which is why McDonagh says "one behaves morally when one responds in an other-centred way; one behaves immorally when one behaves in a self-centred way."[11] The project of morality is to recognize and respond to the call coming forth from another, and to see that call not as a threat or a burden, but as a grace, the key to our freedom from ourselves. In light of McDonagh's analysis of the basic experience and shape of the moral life, we can see why friendship is such a fitting model for it. Friendship begins in recognition of the other, requires appreciation for them precisely as other, and deepens as each moves further out of self and toward the other. In this respect, friendship is a paradigm for moral growth and wholeness.

It is also a paradigm for a different understanding of the self. Friendship is a model for the moral life which insists that the self is social and relational, not autonomous and solitary. When McDonagh argues that our most basic moral experience is being called out of ourselves and into communion with another he is making an argument about what it is to be a self. As recent writings in feminist ethics have insisted, selfhood is not gained by overcoming the other, but by being in relationship with them.[12] Friendship is a model for the moral life especially congenial to feminist ethics because it challenges any view of the person which says individuality is secured only by separating ourselves from others. On this model, selfhood is gained not by being in communion with others, but by standing in opposition to them. Others are not gifts who can enrich us, but obstacles who perduringly frustrate our capacity to be ourself. Harmony can never reign between peoples; hostility is our natural way of being in relation because to the extent that we welcome the other we deny possibilities of ourselves. Like feminist ethics, friendship shifts the basic paradigm of the self, no longer repressing the deep interconnectedness that exists not only between us and all others, but also between us and all life.[13] As Marjorie Suchocki puts it in her essay, "Weaving the World," "Relationships intertwine

our existence. . . . All existence, like our own, is taken to
be constituted through relation and response; all existence
is dynamic; all existence is interdependent through the process of relationship."[14]

Of course, whether we acknowledge the inescapable re-
latedness we have with others largely depends on how we
see them. How do we perceive people very different from
ourselves? The challenge, McDonagh says, is to see the
other person as a gift embodying a call, to see him "as
enriching or at least potentially enriching one's own world.
Any encounter with the world of another has this potential.
Every other man or group comes to one first of all as gift."[15]
The tendency, however, is to see the other not as gift, but
as a threat provoking fear:

> The presence of the other precisely as this different and irre-
> ducible world of its own may also constitute a threat, provok-
> ing fear. There is ample evidence of this from every kind of
> human interchange between groups, whether states or races
> or classes or religions, and between individuals, even individu-
> als in such ostensibly favourable situations as the family or the
> religious community or the Church.[16]

The outcome of our moral life is nestled between these
two possibilities of response. The challenge is to see the
other not as someone alien or frightening, but to behold
them as gift. On the other hand, a perduring human tendency is to see the other not as someone potentially enriching, but as a threat; thus, we react not in hospitality but
in violence.

Consider how we respond to strangers. Is it not true that
often our first impressions of people are wrong? It happens
all the time. We view people defensively, suspiciously, we
evaluate them primarily as unwelcome intrusions upon our
cozy world. Or what about prejudice? Is it not true that at
the bottom of every prejudice, whether racial, ethnic, sex-
ual, or religious, is the perduring refusal to see people quite
other than ourselves as gifts?

We fear certain groups of people because of whatever it is that makes them different from ourselves. We see that difference not as something that could enlarge and enrich our world, but something we fear because we know if we accept it we will be changed. We see the other person as a threat because we both fear and resent the adjustments we must make if we allow them into our lives. We do not welcome them, we refuse to discover there is nothing more interesting than becoming part of another's world. Instead, we view them hostilely, we respond with some sort of violence, often as subtle as ignoring the other, refusing to pay them attention, which is a studied attempt to eliminate them from our world. Everyone of us knows what it is like to be ignored by another, to live or work each day with people who never notice us, who refuse to give us a moment's attention. This hurts because we know when someone refuses to give us attention they implicitly attest that their world is not big enough to include us.[17]

There is often good reason to view another as a threat, or for them to view us this way. Sometimes people make themselves threats instead of gifts. Few people, including ourselves, are ever purely gift or wholly threat. Usually we are a mixture, evoking both trust and fear, anticipation and anxiety, in the lives of those with whom we mingle. The sin in ourselves, in others, and in our world accounts for the element of threat others see in us or we see in them. Even our friends are seldom purely gifts in our lives. They are partially gifts, perhaps primarily gifts, but at some point, through a moment of hurt or betrayal, through some piercing disappointment, they, too, have likely become threats to us. The history of all of our relationships, including our friendships, is a mixture of gift and threat, relationships basically of trust that are occasionally wounded by hurt and unkindness.[18]

That is the fact. The challenge in all our relationships, in every encounter with another, is to allow "the gift to triumph over the threat and so towards enabling the genuine communion and mutual enrichment of the two worlds and not towards the elimination or subordination of one or both."[19] Every relationship is a delicate mixture of gift and threat. In the history of our relationships with others we should work to enable the gift to gain supremacy over the threat, not only to predominate the threat aspect of those relationships, but hopefully, through love, trust, and forgiveness, to move toward elimination of the threat. Short of the Kingdom, a total elimination of the threat is unlikely, but it is toward that love works.

However, in every relationship, even in those which begin as the strongest and most promising gifts in our life, it is easy to allow the threat aspect of the relationship to gain the upper hand. The delicate balance between gift and threat shifts as hurts go unforgiven, as carelessness becomes a way of life. If the threat aspect becomes so overwhelming that the gift seems irremediably lost, as in a divorce, then the relationship breaks down completely. This is why friendships sometimes die.

This is the tragic saga of many relationships and it is real. If morality not only begins in but demands the ongoing capacity to acknowledge and enter the world of another, then despite whatever disappointments and hurts of our life, we must work to allow the gift to triumph over the threat. If the moral life is comprised of the never-ending challenge to move beyond ourself and into the world of another, then we must strive to respond to others in a way that leads to communion and enrichment, not fear and elimination. Put differently, if existence, as the feminists have so rightly insisted, is constitutively relational, then to turn away from others is to begin to disappear. No matter how deep the hurts and disappointments with others have been, to allow the threat to dominate over the gift in our lives is to cease to exist. We cannot be unless we be-in-relationship, that is why we cannot allow threat and fear to prevail; we must work for the love without which we cannot live.

McDonagh next identifies three phases or elements in the subject's response to the other which also mark phases or elements of a friendship. The first phase is recognition.[20] To recognize another is more than seeing them, for indeed we can see them and choose to ignore them. Our recognition of the other has a moral quality because to recognize them is actively to acknowledge the claim they have upon our attention. In the first stage of the moral response, we both experience and acknowledge the call coming forth from another to be attentive to them, to see them as one other than ourself. To recognize them is to experience them impinging on our world and to know we cannot be indifferent to their presence. "The presence of the other as source of particular call," McDonagh says, "awakens the subject to awareness of the call, of the other as source of it, of the subject as subject."[21]

But as we recognize the other, we also recognize ourself. Keeping in mind that the encounter McDonagh describes always occurs between two subjects, our recognition of the other, particularly in their uniqueness and irreducible otherness, allows us to make the same discovery about ourself. McDonagh describes this by saying that other-discovery and self-discovery are interconnected. Our capacity to recognize otherness is directly connected to our capacity to recognize and understand self. Insofar as we can continually welcome the other as gift in our life we discover our own giftedness, we understand why we can be a blessing for them in return.[22] It is in letting their otherness be that we can start to cherish our own.

We can see this in some of the best friendships of our life. One of my best friends, James DeManuele, took the same journey with me to Warrenton, Missouri in the fall of 1965, and is the only other person out of a class of fifty-seven to remain with our community today. If anyone had told us back in 1965 that this was how our journey would evolve, we never would have believed them, not only because we never expected so many to depart, but also because we never expected such an unlikely combination to survive. Jim and I are different in almost every way. With the exception of both being Passionists, everything Jim is I am not, everything I am Jim is not. When we were going through school together, there used to be a joke told about us that captured our differences: people said the two of us together made one interesting person! I am not sure what it meant to them, but, strangely enough, for Jim and me it was a tribute to our friendship. Long ago we realized there was little hope in either of us trying to be the other, we simply were too unlike. Jim has gifts I will never have, I have gifts that will not be his own. We could only be friends, indeed the only way not to drive one another crazy, was to respect each other's uniqueness. We did that, but in doing so we also came to respect ourself. This is what McDonagh means about other-respect being the basis for self-respect. To whatever extent we could celebrate each other's differences, we could embrace and celebrate our own. In whatever way we could recognize how the other could be a gift for us, we could make the same discovery about ourself for him. In learning to love another wildly different from ourself, we learned genuinely to love ourself. In every friendship we experience what McDonagh suggests: our willingness to discover the other leads to fuller discovery of ourself.

There is another side to the experience which McDonagh overlooks and which needs to be emphasized. It is true that much of our sense of self is derived from our capacity to acknowledge the uniqueness of another inasmuch as their uniqueness becomes a reflection of our own, but that is only part of the picture. Some of our identity comes from our recognition of another, but a lot of it comes from how we are recognized by them. So much of who we are is a measure of the attention we have received, so much of how we think of ourself, our appreciation of self, our self-image and identity is other-bestowed. It is exactly this reciprocity that makes friendship so morally important to securing identity.

We gain some sense of self in recognizing another, but we gain more sense of self in being recognized, in being acknowledged and responded to in love. No matter how hard we try to sustain an identity through our overtures toward others, if our recognition is not returned, if we who strive to see are seldom seen, then despite our attempts to reassure ourself of who we are, we begin to doubt we have a self, at least a self worthy of attention. In large measure, how we recognize ourself depends on how we have been recognized and appreciated by others; it depends a lot on our friendships.

This is why kindness is so important. A few years ago I was in Scranton, Pennsylvania. On a Friday afternoon I went for a walk down Main Street. It was November, a chilly, drizzly day. Near the end of my walk I went into a doughnut shop for a cup of coffee. At one end of the large counter sat a few policemen, in the middle was an older man, a poor man, someone obviously down on his luck. I sat down at the far end of the counter, and looked at this man. He was shabbily dressed, dirty; there was nothing about him to make him appealing. It was clear he lived on the streets, making his way through the back alleys of Scranton, asking for handouts, begging for a little change. Like Francis Phelan of William Kennedy's *Ironweed*, he belonged to the "brotherhood of the desolate."[23] Behind the counter that day was a young girl, perhaps seventeen. She worked hard filling orders, but despite how busy she was, she was amazingly cheerful. Throughout the time I was in the coffeeshop, the man was talking to anyone who would listen, but at one point he said, "You know, there is not a day I come in here that she doesn't have a kind word and a smile for me."

I have thought about his comment several times since that afternoon in the doughnut shop. And I suspect he came there each day not just for a cup of coffee, but for the smile and kind word of that girl. I doubt she had any sense what her kindness meant to him. Perhaps it was a small, trifling gesture to her, but it surely was not to him. For someone whose world was the streets, that may well have been the only moment of kind recognition he received. Perhaps it was impossible for her to appreciate the life her smile brought to this man, but to him it was a moment of life, an act of kindness which gifted him with a self he otherwise may not have believed he had. Overlooked, perhaps scorned on the street, this man came to her each day to receive the kindness that kept him alive.

The power of any kindness, of an act of recognition, is that it helps preserve the dignity and identity necessary to being a self. Simone Weil speaks of this in her book, *Waiting for God*. She suggests that all of us are people in waiting; we wait for the attention or recognition of others not just to acknowledge our self or to confirm our self as good, but to gift us with a sense of self only their love can provide. We wait to be befriended. Weil reflects on the plight of lonely people, who always pass unnoticed, whose hour of need passes forever unheeded. She knows the helpless, hopeless situation in which the forever unnoticed find themselves because without the life-giving power of some single kindness, without the prospect of someone to befriend them, they start to feel invisible. Since they seem to exist for no one, they suspect they do not exist at all. As Weil writes, "Those who are unhappy have no need for anything in this world but people capable of giving them their attention."[24]

That is, for all of us, an absolute need. We come to life through the attention of others. The recognition we receive from them is not only life enhancing, it is also life creating, and that is why it is so important that the attention we give another is love. There are people dying for attention, people silently screaming out for a moment of recognition, a chance to be befriended. For us to befriend them is to give them the attention of love, to rescue them with the gift of life sometimes only a stranger can give. More than that, for us to befriend them may give them a sense of self that otherwise they might not have. If the role of the other person is so crucial to our identity, then we must remember that one cannot long go unnoticed and unseen without starting to feel they have no self.

There is an example of this in Mary Gordon's novel, *The Company of Women*. One of the characters is a bitter, mean-spirited woman named Muriel. The housekeeper of Father Cyprian, Muriel generally makes people as forlorn as herself. Everytime Muriel appears in the novel, the reader flinches. She is not a pleasant person, she is complaining, cynical, spiteful. No one wants to be with Muriel, everyone tries to avoid her.

But near the end of the novel, Mary Gordon does something ingenious. She gives each major character a chapter to herself. Felicitas, Charlotte, Clare, each one has the chance for a final word, an opportunity to explain herself without being interrupted or checked by another. Muriel's turn comes, too, and she delivers a surprising message. With rare honesty and numbing sadness, this is how Muriel sees her life:

> My death will be a relief to everybody. There is nothing more lonely than to look among live faces for the face of one who will live after oneself and mourn, the face that, after one's death, will be changed by grief, and to find contempt or an undifferentiated kindness. I wait for a face to meet my face; I wait for the singular gaze, the gaze of permanent choosing, the glance of absolute preferment. This I have always waited for and never found, have hungered for and never tasted. Even now I hope, a woman in a house I cannot sell. I wait here to be looked upon with favor, to be chosen above others, knowing I will die the first beloved of no living soul.[25]

Muriel's tragic estimation of her own life helps us appreciate the role of friendship in the moral life, especially in our own personal development. We see how in friendship, through the loving attention of one who cares for us, we are sculpted into a self. If who we are is so much the work of another's attention, then it is especially the loving attention of our friends wanting what is best for us, devoting themselves to our own good, actively seeking our welfare, even considering us "another self," that forms and shapes us into a person of surprising loveliness. Friends are those who by being lovingly and patiently attentive to us make us into a person we could never have become on our own. Through their painstaking kindness, the studied ways they seek our good, through the artistry of their charity, they bring us into being. Friendship is creative, but it is the friends who create one another, bringing each other to life through the splendor of their love. So often our friends see in us a potential for goodness we cannot see ourself. Through their love for us they bring unsuspected aspects of ourself to life. Or sometimes we can see these possibilities but are not able to touch them. It does not matter. Our friends touch them, our friends draw them out of ourself. Through them we are put in touch with the deepest, most promising aspects of ourself. They lead us to discover ourself in ways we had not known before.

Feminist ethicists can help us understand this point. They argue that if existence is relational, then the friendships and loves of our lives are not something we have, but shapers of who we are. Marjorie Suchocki, after the death of her mother, reflected on the love she had for her. In "Weaving the World," she writes, "The love was not external to me, but rather a name I gave to a certain constitution of myself. Loving my mother became part of my character, one might say. My mother had every reason in the world to 'take it for granted' that I loved her, because the loving had simply become part of who I am."[26] From this experience Suchocki concludes that "everything affects everything else in a relational world," and means by this that the interconnectedness between all of life is so dense that everything we do, all our actions, all our responses, "actually make[s] a difference in the whole of this awesome universe."[27]

How I act toward others affects them not externally but internally, and that means I can render them someone lovely, or I can bruise them deeply. How I relate to others to a large extent determines who they will be. I can touch the promise of their lives and lure it to fullness, or I can crush or destroy them—my agency has that awful, splendid power. If "everything affects everything else in a relational world," quite apart from my intentions, that is the impact of what I do. It is my love which has the power to draw others and the world more fully to life, but it is my hatred, my smallness, my cruelty that also has the power to destroy life. In a world in which "everything affects everything else," my responsibility is that extreme, I can create through my actions but I surely can also destroy.[28] Beverly Wildung Harrison expresses beautifully the awesome power of our actions to create or destroy:

> We do not yet have a moral theology which teaches us the awe-ful, awe-some truth that we have the power through acts of love or lovelessness literally to create one another. I believe that an adequate feminist moral theology must call the tradition of Christian ethics to accountability for minimizing the deep power of human action in the work of or the denial of love. Because we do not understand love as the power to act-each-other-into-well-being we also do not understand the depth of our power to thwart life and to maim each other. The fateful choice is ours, either to set free the power of God's love in the world or to deprive each other of the very basis of personhood and community.[29]

If so much of who we are is the work of another's love, then an integral aspect of Christian friendship is to take time to be attentive and responsive to all those so consistently overlooked and forgotten that they depend on us to preserve for them the basic human dignity of being a self. Perhaps the crucial test case for Christian friendship is our willingness to nurture for another a self they never were allowed to believe they had. In this respect Christian friendship is everyday Christian ministry.

But perhaps even more important than the recognition we give them is our willingness to receive and confirm the recognition they may so desperately want to give us. This, too, is part of Christian friendship. There is no better way to affirm the value and worth of another person, no surer sign of our affirmation of their goodness, than to be willing to receive the offer of their attention as a gift. Sometimes, perhaps surprisingly, it is our willingness to be available to their love that leads to some of the richest and most powerful moral experiences of our lives. It at least reminds us that we are often most blessed when we receive another very different from ourself as gift. As the judgment scene in Matthew 25 attests, Jesus, the ultimate gift in our lives, sometimes comes cloaked in the guise of a threat.

The second phase of the moral encounter described by McDonagh is respect.[30] Respect is a kind of patience. To respect another person is to take whatever time is necessary to see their goodness. Respect literally means to "look again," to "take a second look." It means we cannot settle for first impressions, or casually dismiss people from our lives. To have respect for someone is to look far enough into the person to see their goodness, even if that goodness is more a promise than a fact. We respect them when we call them to this goodness and commit ourself to eliciting it. Respect often takes the form of patience because it is not always easy to see this goodness, and sometimes a person neither recognizes nor lives according to it themself; hence to pledge ourself to respect means we take whatever time is necessary to spot the goodness to which God calls them. In this way, respect is an element of justice because to be patient enough to find another's goodness is to do for another what God does for us all.

As other-recognition leads to self-recognition, McDonagh says other-respect enables self-respect. "Recognition and acceptance of the value of others enables one to recognise and accept the value of the self," McDonagh writes. "Self-acceptance and self-respect will be as real and effective as one's other-acceptance and other-respect."[31] We can be self-accepting to the degree that we are other-accepting, and the more we are able to respect another, to see them in their most promising goodness, the more we are able to respect the dignity and worth uniquely our own.

All this seems true enough; however, it also seems true that in a large measure we can have self-respect only if we have experienced ourself being respected by others. It is much easier to see another's goodness when we know others have recognized and responded to our own. It is much easier to take the risk of loving someone when we know we are loved and cherished by another. Friendship looms large here because friendship is the nurturing, caring relationship in which we are accepted and respected for who we are, respected for our self in our own inviolable dignity and preciousness. Our friends tell us we are someone important to them; in fact, they tell us we are so valuable and enriching for their lives that they cannot imagine themselves without us, that is why they speak of us as "another self." To be deemed such is a high form of respect, unexcelled witness of the goodness other people see in us. For them to acknowledge us as friend is to acknowledge us as a blessing for their lives. Their esteem for who we are, their investment in us, enables self-respect. It is our friends' affirmation of our goodness that enables us to enlarge our world by welcoming others into it. Assured of our own worth, we are willing to help others find it in themselves.

The third phase in the encounter with another is response.[32] Our recognition and respect for another prompts us to reach out to them in response. The manner of this response will vary according to the person before us and the situation in which we find ourself. As McDonagh says, "It can obviously take innumerable different forms from a reassuring smile of recognition to laying down one's life for the other ."[33] But in every instance the response involves a moving out of ourself to another. To reach out in response is to break free from the confinement of our own world and, if only momentarily, to enter the world of the other. It is an instance of breaking boundaries so that two previously separate worlds can become one.

There is a twofold movement in this response, as there is in the forming of every friendship. The first instant of love, and indeed an experience in the formation and development of a friendship, is a momentary loss of self which occurs as we move beyond the isolation of the self into communion with another. "This self-transcedence to reach the other as other involves a certain disintegration of the world of the self including its previous settled relationship to the other,"[34] McDonagh says. There is a disintegration of the self in friendship because there is also a redefinition of self. We are no longer defined strictly in terms of our self, but in relation to another.

But love does not stop with disintegration, it moves toward communion. That is why we seek friendship. The only thing which enables us to risk surpassing our self is the promise of rich and fuller life with another. Ultimately, the gift in the other triumphs over the threat because our desire for life together, this hunger for communion, is stronger than the fear which keeps us apart. It is exactly because we do not want to be alone that the threat aspect in all of us will not prevail. Indeed, this is ultimately the work of God's love, but that only attests to the deepest truth about us: we both need and seek the union of ourself with another. As McDonagh puts it, "But this should then issue in a reintegration of subject and relationship at a deeper level of communion achieved through the reaching out in recognition, respect, and response, and at a deeper level of differentiation, achieved for the subject in a fuller self-identification, self-acceptance, and self-creation."[35]

Why self-creation? Because our response to another leads to fuller development of ourself. In McDonagh's parlance, other-response is self-developing.[36] When we reach out toward others we bring new features of ourself into existence. Each time we do respond we fashion some aspect of ourself. Our creative response to all the people who pass through our life is also creative of self. Nothing does more for us than the kindness we expend on another. What the Gospel says is true: we really are happiest and most fulfilled when we are able to forget ourself and focus on the need of another. Our purest happiness comes in those rare moments of self-forgetfulness when we are so taken up in doing good for another that we are, however briefly, freed from anxious concern for ourself. Kindness, generosity, self-giving are eminently creative both for others and for ourself. Strangely enough, the more we give ourself to developing another, the more, often unbeknownst to ourself, we develop ourself. Our kindness has a way of coming back to us, of shaping us in the same love and goodness we offer another.

III. Conclusion

What McDonagh's analysis shows this book has tried to echo. The premise of this book is that the moral life is not a solitary enterprise, but is what happens to us in relationship to others, especially the friendship relationships most crucial to our lives. As Aristotle taught us, to speak of the moral life as friendship is to acknowledge both how the self is formed and how we achieve the good for which we are made. As Aquinas's analysis of charity suggested, the purpose of life is to achieve a union with God based on likeness to God, and this transfiguration of the self unto God occurs in those friendships in which Christ is also found. Such friendships are constitutive of the Christian moral life because it is only in company with those who share our desire to gain God that we learn the love God is. And as our study of Augustine, Aelred of Rievaulx, and Karl Barth intimated, it is not a love that shrivels up our world, hardly a love that makes our world smaller; rather, it is a love of such exquisite, demanding generosity that it looks upon all, even the enemy, as friend. When the good to be gained is God, we have a friendship which opens us to the world.

Those of us who left our homes for Warrenton in the fall of 1965 did embark on an adventure from which we never fully recovered, but that is our hope and I suspect it remains our joy. It was an adventure in friendship, a glorying in the good we found in Christ. Perhaps that is why we remember it so fondly, perhaps that is why it shaped us in ways we hope not to lose. Though we could not articulate it then, the power of Warrenton was that it strove to make a single possibility real; it offered us a way of life in which all of us infants of God could become the friends of God. The plot of the Christian moral life is to enable the same, to seize that singular possibility and make it real. It is an amazing adventure because it fits us for a Kingdom whose goodness and joy brings a peace we can never exhaust. Out in that Missouri countryside we found a memory from which a hope continues to be born, and it is this: The Christian moral life is what happens to us when we grant God, and others, the freedom to be our friends.

Notes

1. Friendship and the Moral Life

1. The finest account of this description of our contemporary moral landscape is Alasdair MacIntyre's *After Virtue* (Notre Dame, Ind.: University of Notre Dame Press, 1981), esp. pp. 1–34.

2. Bernard Williams, *Ethics and the Limits of Philosophy* (Cambridge, Mass.: Harvard University Press, 1985), p. 4. As Williams writes in the opening paragraph of this book: "It is not a trivial question, Socrates said: what we are talking about is how one should live. Or so Plato reports him, in one of the first books written about this subject. Plato thought that philosophy could answer the question. . . . The aims of moral philosophy, and any hopes it may have of being worth serious attention, are bound up with the fate of Socrates' first question, even if it is not true that philosophy, itself, can reasonably hope to answer it" p. 1.

3. *Ethics and the Limits of Philosophy*, pp. 4–5. Near the end of the chapter Williams adds: "Once constituted in that way, it very naturally moves from the question asked by anybody, 'how should I live?' to the question 'how should anybody live?' That seems to ask for the reasons we all share for living in one way rather than another. It seems to ask for the conditions of the good life—the right life, perhaps, for human beings as such" p. 20.

4. *Optatan Totius*, 17. Vatican Council II, *The Conciliar and Post Conciliar Documents*, ed. Austin Flannery, O.P. (Collegeville, Minn.: Liturgical Press, 1975).

5. Graham Greene, *The Power and the Glory* (New York: Penguin Books, 1982), p. 210.

168

6. Josef Pieper, *On Hope* (San Francisco: Ignatius Press, 1986), p. 28.

7. Stanley Hauerwas, *The Peaceable Kingdom* (Notre Dame, Ind.: University of Notre Dame Press, 1983), p. 3.

8. Iris Murdoch, "Against Dryness: A Polemical Sketch," *Revisions: Changing Perspectives in Moral Philosophy,* ed. Stanley Hauerwas and Alasdair MacIntyre (Notre Dame, Ind.: University of Notre Dame Press, 1983), p. 44.

9. Ibid., p. 46.

10. Robert N. Bellah et al., *Habits of the Heart* (Berkeley, Calif.: University of California Press, 1985), p. 76.

11. Murdoch, "Against Dryness," p. 49.

12. Edmund Pincoffs, "Quandary Ethics," *Changing Perspectives in Moral Philosophy,* ed. Stanley Hauerwas and Alasdair MacIntyre (Notre Dame, Ind.: University of Notre Dame Press, 1983), p. 93.

13. Hauerwas, *The Peaceable Kingdom,* p. 116.

14. Ibid., p. 117.

15. Ibid.

16. Ibid.

17. Stanley Hauerwas, *A Community of Character: Toward A Constructive Christian Social Ethic* (Notre Dame, Ind.: University of Notre Dame Press, 1981), pp. 114–115. For a similar emphasis on the connection between character and moral assessment, see Gilbert C. Meilander, *The Theory and Practice of Virtue* (Notre Dame, Ind.: University of Notre Dame Press, 1984), esp. pp. 45–99; and Craig Dykstra, *Vision and Character: A Christian Educator's Alternative to Kohlberg* (New York: Paulist Press, 1981), esp. pp. 33–62.

18. Pincoffs, "Quandary Ethics," p. 101.

19. Ibid., p. 105.

20. Ibid., p. 93.

21. Ibid.

22. Ibid., p. 94.

23. Ibid., p. 95.

24. Etienne Gilson, *Moral Values and the Moral Life: The System of St. Thomas Aquinas* (Saint Louis: B. Herder Book Co., 1931), p. 19.

25. Paul L. Holmer, *Making Christian Sense* (Philadelphia: Westminster Press, 1984), p. 20.

2. A Look at Aristotle's Ethics

1. Walker Percy, *Love in the Ruins* (New York: Avon Books, 1971), p. 18.
2. Ibid., p. 7.
3. Ibid., p. 188.
4. Ibid., p. 181.
5. Ibid., p. 20.
6. Ibid., p. 131.
7. Ibid.
8. MacIntyre, *After Virtue*, p. 1.
9. Ibid., p. 1.
10. Ibid., p. 21.
11. Ibid., p. 57.
12. Ibid., p. 2.
13. Ibid., pp. 49–75.
14. Ibid., p. 111.
15. One of the best treatments of how Aristotle envisioned the moral life, particularly the notion that morality involves a way of life which makes possible a particular understanding of human fullness, is Stuart Hampshire's *Morality and Conflict* (Cambridge, Mass.: Harvard University Press, 1983), esp. pp. 10–45.
16. MacIntyre, *After Virtue*, p. 112.
17. Ibid., p. 51. For MacIntyre, it was precisely the Enlightenment project's rejection of a "teleological view of human nature, any view of man as having an essence which defines his true end," that explains "why their project of finding a basis for morality had to fail." Once the teleological framework for traditional moral injunctions had been denied, the intelligibility of those injunctions was strained; it simply was impossible to offer a coherent account for why people should or should not do certain things since the goals and purposes in light of which those positions could be understood had been rejected.
18. J. L. Ackrill, "Aristotle on Eudaimonia," in *Essays on Aristotle's Ethics,* ed. Amelie Oksenberg Rorty (Berkeley, Calif.: University of California Press, 1980), p. 24.
19. Aristotle, *Nichomachaen Ethics,* tr. Martin Ostwald (Indianapolis: Bobbs-Merrill Educational Publishing Co., 1962), 1094a18.

20. *NE* 1097a19.

21. *NE* 1097a29–1097b5. Ostwald translates 'eudaimonia' as happiness, but we have noted the problems with this translation.

22. Ackrill, "Aristotle on Eudaimonia," p. 22.

23. Ibid.

24. Ibid., p. 26.

25. Ibid., p. 21.

26. Ibid., p. 22.

27. *NE* 1097a29.

28. Ackrill, "Aristotle on Eudaimonia," p. 26.

29. Ibid., p. 28.

30. Ibid., p. 21.

31. Ibid.

32. *NE* 1097b15.

33. Ackrill, "Aristotle on Eudaimonia," p. 24.

34. *NE* 1095b16.

35. Julia Annas, "Aristotle on Pleasure and Goodness," in *Essays on Aristotle's Ethics*, ed. Amelie Oksenberg Rorty (Berkeley, Calif.: University of California Press, 1980), p. 288.

36. Ibid., p. 288.

37. Ibid., p. 289. See also MacIntyre, *After Virtue*, p. 140.

38. *NE* 1099b15.

39. *NE* 1099b26. Aristotle is enough of a realist to know that even though eudaimonia is constituted by the virtuous life, it must be accompanied by a sufficient amount of external goods to make that life possible. One needs an adequate amount of wealth, material goods, and leisure possibilities to cultivate the virtues (N 1099a31–1099b8). This is exactly why Aristotle takes good luck and bad luck, fortune and misfortune, so seriously. Thus, Aristotle offers this summary definition of eudaimonia: "Is there anything to prevent us, then, from defining the happy man as one whose activities are an expression of complete virtue, and who is sufficiently equipped with external goods, not simply at a given moment but to the end of his life?" (NE 1101a14–16).

40. Ackrill, "Aristotle on Eudaimonia," p. 24.

41. Ibid., p. 27.

42. MacIntyre suggests Aristotle's insistence that the genuinely virtuous person has all the virtues in their complete form—

his emphasis on the unity and interconnection of the virtues—
reflects both the ahistorical nature of much of his writing as well
as his inability to accept conflict as an ineliminable part of the
moral life, that is, his inability to see tragedy as sometimes being
an aspect of our life in the world and not just a manifestation of
some flaw in character. See *After Virtue*, pp. 147–153.

43. MacIntyre, *After Virtue*, pp. 139–140.

44. *NE* 1097b25–27.

45. Thomas Nagel, "Aristotle on Eudaimonia," in *Essays on Aristotle's Ethics*, ed. Amelie Oksenberg Rorty (Berkeley, Calif.: University of California Press, 1980), p. 8.

46. *NE* 1098a12–16.

47. MacIntyre, *After Virtue*, p. 163.

48. *NE* 1153a1.

3. Aristotle on Friendship

1. *NE* 1094b7.

2. MacIntyre, *After Virtue*, p. 146.

3. Ibid.

4. Ibid.

5. Gilbert C. Meilaender makes this point in his book, *Friendship: A Study in Theological Ethics* (Notre Dame, Ind.: University of Notre Dame Press, 1981), p. 70.

6. *NE* 1180a26.

7. *NE* 1180a25.

8. *NE* 1180a29–32.

9. *NE* 1181b25. I am grateful to David B. Burrell of the University of Notre Dame for this insight.

10. MacIntyre, *After Virtue*, p. 244.

11. Ibid., p. 245.

12. John M. Cooper, "Aristotle on Friendship," in *Essays on Aristotle's Ethics*, ed. Amelie Oksenberg Rorty (Berkeley, Calif.: University of California Press, 1980), p. 303.

13. *NE* 1156a10–14.

14. *NE* 1156a15–24.

15. Cooper, "Aristotle on Friendship," p. 308.

16. *NE* 1056b24.

17. *NE* 1055b30.

18. *NE* 1056b6–22.

19. Cooper, "Aristotle on Friendship," p. 304.

20. Ibid.

21. Ibid.

22. Ibid., p. 305.

23. Ibid., p. 308.

24. Ibid., p. 304.

25. Ibid., p. 305.

26. Ibid.

27. Ibid., p. 309.

28. Martha C. Nussbaum, *The Fragility of Goodness* (Cambridge: Cambridge University Press, 1986), p. 355.

29. Ibid., pp. 355–356.

30. Cooper, "Aristotle on Friendship," p. 318.

31. Ibid., p. 322.

32. Cooper cautions that "the motif of the friend as a mirror, which is indeed at best implicit in the *Nichomachean* argument, is not to be interpreted as meaning that on Aristotle's view a flourishing person treats his friend as a mere instrument by which to enhance his own self-esteem. On the contrary, this image implies that his self-esteem only gets the support he seeks insofar as he first has precisely the same esteem for the other person and his life, taken by itself, as he will come to have for himself and his own life," "Aristotle on Friendship," p. 333. With this qualification Cooper avoids the friend being used as nothing more than an opportunity for our self-knowledge. As he stresses, it is only when we love and value the friend for his sake that we can, in turn, learn to appreciate ourselves.

33. Cooper, "Aristotle on Friendship," p. 324.

34. Ibid., p. 322.

35. Ibid., p. 329.

36. Ibid., pp. 329–330.

37. Ibid., p. 327.

38. Ibid., p. 325.

39. Ibid., p. 327.

40. The argument that we need good friends, friends of virtue and character, is implicit in Cooper's remark that it is "only with such persons" that we can share and flourish in those

activities most central to our life. He remarks, "Hence, a human being cannot have a flourishing life except by having intimate friends to whom he is attached precisely on account of their good qualities of character and who are similarly attached to him: it is only with such persons tht he can share the moral activities that are most central to his life," "Aristotle on Friendship," p. 330.

41. *NE* 1155a3–4.
42. *NE* 1170a11–12.
43. *NE* 1171b31–1172a7.
44. *NE* 1159b29–30.
45. *NE* 1159b32.
46. *NE* 1169b4–8.
47. *NE* 1169b8–10.
48. *NE* 1169b11–14.
49. *NE* 1169b28.
50. *NE* 1170a2.
51. *NE* 1172a5–8.
52. *NE* 1172a11–13.
53. Percy, *Love in the Ruins,* p. 36.
54. Ibid., p. 37.
55. Ibid., p. 175.
56. Ibid., p. 178.

4. Friendship as Preferential Love

1. Meilaender, *Friendship,* p. 2.
2. For an excellent methodological study of Christian love or agape, see Gene Outka, *Agape: An Ethical Analysis* (New Haven, Conn.: Yale University Press, 1972).
3. Meilaender, *Friendship,* p. 3.
4. Ibid., p. 7.
5. An excellent account of how our understanding of certain concepts depends on the narrative and tradition in which they are placed is Alasdair MacIntyre's "The Virtues, the Unity of a Human Life and the Concept of a Tradition," *After Virtue,* pp. 190–209. See also "From System to Story: An Alternative Pattern for Rationality in Ethics," Stanley Hauerwas, with David

B. Burrell, *Truthfulness and Tragedy* (Notre Dame, Ind.: University of Notre Dame Press, 1977), pp. 15–39.

6. Soren Kierkegaard, *Works of Love,* trans. Howard and Edna Hong (New York: Harper & Row, 1964), p. 58.

7. Ibid., p. 63.

8. Ibid., p. 65.

9. Ibid., pp. 65–66.

10. Ibid., p. 66.

11. Ibid., pp. 68–70.

12. Ibid., p. 70. Kierkegaard bases this assessment of neighbor love on a claim about the Divine love according to which human love must be gauged. It is because "in God there is no partiality" (p. 74) that Kierkegaard reasons we truly love our neighbors only when we make "not the slightest distinction" between them. His claim about neighbor love is based on a claim about God's love; however, what Kierkegaard does not see is that for God to love all people does not mean God must love without partiality or distinction; indeed, it would seem love requires making distinctions since to love someone demands seeing clearly his or her uniqueness, seeing what makes him or her different, and, therefore, uniquely lovable.

13. Lawrence A. Blum, *Friendship, Altruism, and Morality* (London: Routledge & Kegan Paul, 1980), p. 70.

14. Ibid.

15. Ibid., p. 75.

16. Kierkegaard, *Works of Love,* pp. 112–113.

17. Ibid., p. 117.

18. Anders Nygren, *Agape and Eros,* trans. Philip S. Watson (New York: Harper & Row, Publishers, 1969), p. 48.

19. Ibid., p. 63.

20. A similar argument is advanced in Stanley Hauerwas's "Love's Not All You Need," *Vision and Virtue* (Notre Dame, Ind.: University of Notre Dame Press, 1974), pp. 111–126.

21. Ibid., p. 114.

22. Nygren, *Agape and Eros,* p. 156.

23. Ibid., pp. 66–67.

24. David B. Burrell, "Religious Belief and Rationality," in *Rationality and Religious Belief,* ed. C. F. Delaney (Notre Dame, Ind.: University of Notre Dame Press, 1979), p. 100. See also

Kenneth Sayre, "A Perceptual Model of Belief in God," in *The Autonomy of Religious Belief*, ed. Frederick Crosson (Notre Dame, Ind.: University of Notre Dame Press, 1981), pp. 108–127, and Paul L. Holmer, *The Grammar of Faith* (San Francisco: Harper & Row, 1978).

25. Nygren, *Agape and Eros*, p. 66.
26. Ibid., p. 75.
27. Ibid.
28. Ibid.
29. Ibid., p. 76.
30. Ibid., pp. 75–76.
31. Ibid., p. 77.
32. Ibid.
33. Ibid.
34. Ibid.
35. Ibid., p. 78.
36. Ibid., p. 80.
37. Ibid., p. 78.
38. Ibid., p. 80.
39. Ibid., p. 92.
40. Ibid., p. 93.
41. Ibid., pp. 101–102.
42. Ibid., p. 96.
43. Ibid., pp. 96–97.
44. Ibid., p. 97.
45. Ibid., p. 153.
46. Ibid., p. 154.
47. Ibid.
48. Augustine, *The Confessions*, trans. John K. Ryan (Garden City, N.J.: Image Books, 1960), IV:4, p. 97.
49. Ibid.
50. Marie Aquinas McNamara, O.P., *Friendship in Saint Augustine* (Fribourg: University Press, 1958), p. 196.
51. See Meilaender, *Friendship*, pp. 16–17.
52. McNamara, *Friendship in Saint Augustine*, pp. 196–197.
53. Ibid., p. 202.
54. See Meilaender, *Friendship*, p. 21.
55. *Confessions*, IV:4, p. 97.
56. McNamara, *Friendship in Saint Augustine*, p. 206.

57. Ibid., p. 197.
58. Ibid., p. 199.
59. Ibid., p. 200.
60. See Oliver O'Donovan, *The Problem of Self-Love in St. Augustine* (New Haven, Conn.: Yale University Press, 1980), pp. 129–130.
61. Meilaender, *Friendship,* p. 17.
62. Ibid., p. 66.
63. Ibid.
64. Ibid., p. 21.
65. Ibid., pp. 34–35.
66. McNamara, *Friendship in Saint Augustine,* p. 221.
67. Ibid., p. 222.
68. Ibid., p. 223.
69. Ibid., p. 222.
70. From Augustine's *Commentary on the Gospel of John,* cited in *Friendship in Saint Augustine,* p. 221.
71. Aelred of Rievaulx, *Spiritual Friendship,* trans. Mary Eugenia Laker, SSND, with an introduction by Douglas Roby (Kalamazoo, Mich.: Cistercian Publications, 1977), p. 10. I am grateful to Placid Solari, OSB, for bringing this work to my attention.
72. Ibid., Prologue, 2.
73. Ibid., Prologue, 4.
74. Ibid., 2:9.
75. Ibid., 1:38.
76. The supremacy of spiritual friendship is seen in the strikingly different descriptions Aelred gives the various kinds of friendship. About carnal friendship he says: "The real beginning of carnal friendship proceeds from an affection which like a harlot directs its step after every passer-by, following its own lustful ears and eyes in every direction." In carnal friendship, "spirit is captivated by spirit, and one is inflamed by the other, and they are kindled to form a sinful bond, so that, after they have entered upon such a deplorable pact, the one will do or suffer any crime or sacrilege whatsoever for the sake of the other" (1:39–40). Worldly friendship is only slightly better: "But worldly friendship, which is born of a desire for temporal advantage or possessions, is always full of deceit and intrigue; it con-

tains nothing certain, nothing constant, nothing secure; for, to be sure, it ever changes with fortune and follows the purse" (1:42). Finally, spiritual friendship: "For spiritual friendship, which we call true, should be desired, not for consideration of any worldly advantage or for any extrinsic cause, but from the dignity of its own nature and the feelings of the human heart, so that its fruition and reward is nothing other than itself. . . . And so spiritual friendship among the just is born of a similarity in life, morals, and pursuits, that is, it is a mutual conformity in matters human and divine united with benevolence and charity" (1:45–46).

77. *Spiritual Friendship*, 3:5.
78. Ibid., 1:1.
79. Ibid., 1:8.
80. Ibid., 1:9.
81. Ibid., 2:20–21.
82. Ibid., 2:14.
83. Ibid., 1:21.
84. Ibid., 3:134.
85. Ibid., 3:79–80.
86. Karl Barth, *Church Dogmatics,* vol. IV, part 2, "The Doctrine of Reconciliation," trans. Rev. G. W. Bromiley (Edinburgh: T. & T. Clark, 1958), p. 733.
87. Ibid., p. 733.
88. Ibid., p. 734.
89. Ibid., p. 733–734. That Barth sees self-giving to be the distinguishing mark of Christian love is based on his understanding of God's Trinitarian love. It is because the love of God is characterized essentially by self-giving that Christians are called to love likewise. See p. 757.
90. Barth, *Church Dogmatics,* vol. IV, part 2, p. 745.
91. Ibid., p. 752.
92. Ibid.
93. Ibid., p. 753.
94. Ibid.
95. Ibid., p. 778
96. Ibid., p. 752.
97. Ibid., p. 804.
98. Ibid., p. 805.
99. Ibid., p. 809.

100. Ibid.
101. Ibid., pp. 806–807.
102. Ibid., p. 814.
103. Ibid., p. 812.
104. Ibid., p. 813.
105. Ibid.
106. Ibid., pp. 815–816.
107. Ibid., p. 809.

5. The Christian Life as Friendship with God

1. Thomas Aquinas, *Summa Theologiae*, I-II, 65,5. The text of the *Summa Theologiae* used is the Blackfriar's edition, ed. Thomas Gilby, O.P. (New York: McGraw-Hill Book Co., 1963–1969).

2. Percy, *Love in the Ruins*, p. 37.

3. Richard Egenter, *Gottesfreundschaft: Die Lehre von der Gottesfreundschaft in der Scholastik und Mystik des 12, und 13. Jahrhunderts* (Augsburg: Dr. Benno Filser, 1928), p. 43.

4. *ST*, II-II, 23,1.

5. *ST*, I-II, 3,2.

6. Joseph Keller, "De Virtute Caritatis Ut Amicitia Quadam Divina," *Xenia Thomistica Theologica* 2 (1925): p. 248.

7. *ST*, II-II, 24,2.

8. Aquinas, *Summa Contra Gentiles*, Book III, Part II, trans. Vernon J. Bourke (Notre Dame, Ind.: University of Notre Dame Press, 1975), III, 2, c. 150.

9. *ST*, I-II, 110,2.

10. *ST*, I-II, 109,9.

11. *NE* 1156b32–35.

12. *NE* 1156b6–7.

13. I am grateful to Dan Nelson for bringing this question to my attention and for posing it so clearly.

14. *ST*, II-II, 23,1.

15. See J. E. Van Roey, "De Charitate Forma Virtutum," *Ephemerides Theologicae Louvaniensis* 1 (1924): p. 47.

16. *ST*, I-II, 3,2.

17. *ST*, I-II, 3,2.

18. See R. Guindon, *Beátitude et Théologie Morale Chez St. Thomas D'Aquin* (Ottawa: Editions de l'Universite d'Ottawa, 1956), p. 296.

19. *ST,* I-II, 65,5.

20. *ST,* II-II, 23,1.

21. E. Neveut, "La Vertu De Charité: Son Caractère Surnaturel," *Divus Thomas* 40 (1937): p. 145.

22. *ST,* I-II, 26,4.

23. Henri Noble, *L'Amitié Avec Dieu* (Paris: Desclée et Cie, 1932), p. 24.

24. *ST,* II-II, 23,1.

25. Robert O. Johann, *The Meaning of Love* (Glen Rock, N.J.: Paulist Press, 1966), pp. 46–47.

26. Paul Philippe, *Le Rôle de L'Amitié Dans La Vie Chrétienne Selon Saint Thomas D'Aquin* (Rome: Angelicum, 1938), pp. 29–30.

27. *NE* 1157b18–20.

28. *NE* 1171b31–1172a3.

29. Aquinas, *Scriptum Super Sententiis Magistri Petri Lombardi* (Paris: P. Lethielleux, 1933), III, d. 27, q. 2, a. 1.

30. *Scriptum Super Sententiis Magistri Petri Lombardi,* III, d. 27, q. 2, a. 1.

31. Interestingly, in the early part of this century, this notion of charity as a sharing of life with God that becomes a conversion of the self to God, was the center of a dispute. For one side of the argument, see M. Coconnier, "Ce Qu'Est La Charité d'Après St. Thomas d'Aquin," *Revue Thomiste* 14 (1906): pp. 5–30. For the other, see Joseph Keller and Benoit Lavaud, "La Charité Comme Amitié d'Après S. Thomas," *Revue Thomiste* 12 (1929): pp. 445–475. Keller and Lavaud claimed that Coconnier said what is communicated in charity is not the Spirit, but the society or fellowship of friendship itself. If this is what Coconnier meant, he was clearly mistaken. Yet, in his much disputed article of 1906 Coconnier did distinguish between the offering of God's love with which charity begins, and the sharing of life in which it is sustained. He insisted both are necessary to have a friendship.

32. Aquinas, *Summa Contra Gentiles.* Book Three: Providence, Part 1, trans. Vernon J. Bourke (Notre Dame, Ind.: University of Notre Dame Press, 1975), 3, c. 19.

33. Henri Noble, "L'Amitié De La Charité," *La vie Spiri-tuelle,* 12 (1925): p. 11.

34. See Keller, "De Virtute Caritatis ut Amicitia Quadam Divina," p. 256.

35. H. D. Simonin, "Autour De La Solution Thomiste Du Probleme De L'Amour," *Archives d'Histoire Doctrinale et Litteraire du Moyen Age,* VI (1931), pp. 265–266.

36. Egenter, *Gottesfreundschaft,* p. 40.

37. A similar position is found in Tibor Horvath's *Caritas Est in Ratione* (Munster: Aschendorff, 1966), p. 167.

38. Jean Mourous, *The Christian Experience,* trans. George Lamb (New York: Sheed and Ward, 1954), pp. 263–264. I am grateful to Fred Sucher, C.P., for bringing this book to my attention.

6. Friendship and Everyday Life

1. Thomas W. Ogletree, *Hospitality To The Stranger* (Philadelphia: Fortress Press, 1985), p. 46.

2. Ibid., pp. 2–3. Later in the book, Ogletree speaks of a "hermeneutics of hospitality," and describes it "as a readiness to welcome strange and unfamiliar meanings into our own awareness, perhaps to be shaken by them, but in no case to be left unchanged. These meanings enable us to become aware of limitations in the concrete historicity of our own view of things. We always come to situations with our particular understandings, our prejudices Gadamer calls them, when we begin to interpret" (p. 119).

3. Ogletree, *Hospitality To The Stranger,* p. 45.

4. Ibid., p. 35.

5. Tennessee Williams, *A Streetcar Named Desire* (New York: New Directions Publishing Corporation, 1980), p. 178.

6. Enda McDonagh, *Gift and Call* (Saint Meinrad, Ind.: Abbey Press, 1975), pp. 29–30.

7. Ibid., p. 28.

8. Ibid., p. 27.

9. Ibid., pp. 30–31.

10. Ibid., p. 30

11. Ibid., p. 33.

12. See especially Catherine Keller, *From A Broken Web* (Boston: Beacon Press, 1986), pp. 1–46, and "Feminism and the Ethic of Inseparability," in *Women's Consciousness and Women's Conscience,* ed. Barbara Hilkert Andolsen, Christine E. Gudorf, and Mary D. Pellauer (San Francisco: Harper & Row, 1985), p. 254.

13. See Ruth L. Smith, "Feminism and the Moral Subject," in *Women's Consciousness and Women's Conscience,* p. 236.

14. Majorie Suchocki, "Weaving the World," *Process Studies* 14 (1985): p. 80.

15. McDonagh, *Gift and Call,* p. 34.

16. Ibid., p. 36.

17. Ibid.

18. Ibid., pp. 36–37.

19. Ibid., p. 37.

20. Ibid., p. 43.

21. Ibid., p. 44.

22. Ibid., p. 45.

23. William Kennedy, *Ironweed* (New York: Penquin Books, 1984), p. 23.

24. Simone Weil, *Waiting for God,* trans. Emma Craufurd (New York: Harper & Row, 1973), p. 114.

25. Mary Gordon, *The Company of Women* (New York: Ballantine Books, 1980), p. 275.

26. Suchocki, "Weaving The World," p. 79.

27. Ibid., p. 81.

28. Ibid.

29. Beverly Wildung Harrison, "The Power of Anger in the Work of Love: Christian Ethics for Women and Other Strangers," *Union Seminary Quarterly Review* 36 (1980–81): p. 47.

30. McDonagh, *Gift and Call,* p. 49.

31. Ibid., p. 50

32. Ibid., p. 57.

33. Ibid.

34. Ibid., p. 61.

35. Ibid.

36. Ibid., p. 58.

Index